The Great Rotisserie Chicken Cookbook

THE GREAT

ROTISSERIE

CHICKEN

COOKBOOK

More than 100 Delicious Ways to Enjoy
Storebought and Homecooked Chicken

ERIC AKIS

appetite

by RANDOM HOUSE

Copyright © 2015 Eric Akis

Appetite by Random House® colophon is a registered trademark

Library and Archives of Canada Cataloguing in Publication Data is available upon request

ISBN: 978-0-449-01640-4
eBook ISBN: 978-0-449-01641-1

Cover and food photography: Jo-Ann Richards, Works Photography
Food preparation and styling: Eric Akis
Copy editing: Naomi Pauls
Proofreading and indexing: Lana Okerlund

Printed and bound in China

Published in Canada by Appetite by Random House®,
a division of Random House of Canada Limited

www.penguinrandomhouse.ca

10 9 8 7 6 5 4 3 2 1

appetite
by RANDOM HOUSE | Penguin
Random
House

CONTENTS

Acknowledgments

This is my eighth cookbook, and once again I've learned that producing one is a team sport. Without key players in the right positions and support from people who care, creating a book of this quality just isn't possible.

Thank you to Appetite by Random House Publisher and cookbook guru Robert McCullough for selecting me for this project. It was a thrill and an honor to work with you again. You truly inspire me!

To editor Lucy Kenward, thank you for helping me turn this book's contents from good to great. You pushed me to reach heights I didn't know I could reach, and I feel very good about that. To editor Lindsay Paterson and designer Kelly Hill, thank you for your skilled assistance in the planning stages of this book. And thank you to designer Jennifer Lum. You took everyone's input, combined it with your own vision, and created a beautiful-looking, uscr-fricndly book.

To Jo-Ann Richards, owner of Works Photography in Victoria, B.C., thank you for taking the fabulous photos in this book. And thank you for being so enthusiastic, for approaching each image with artistic consideration, and for being so flexible with scheduling. You are a superstar!

To Graham Smyth and Michelle Smith, proprietors of Bungalow, a splendid gift and cookware store in Victoria, B.C., and to Susan Lewis, a forever friend and stalwart supporter of my culinary adventures, thank you for lending me much of the fine tableware, boards, platters, and linens used to showcase the great recipes in this book.

To my wife, Cheryl, and son, Tyler, who have always considered "chicken dinner" to be the very best family meal, you both know the time and effort that's involved in creating a book like this and without your love and shoulders to lean on I would not have reached the finish line. Thank you.

Why Choose a Rotisserie Chicken?

If you like the flavor of chicken, rotisserie cooking turns that feeling to love. As the chicken spins around on the spit, its whole exterior takes on the most marvelously rich, I-want-to-eat-you-now color and its juices reach every part of the bird, making the meat succulent and ultra-moist. If your taste buds are already tingling, they'll go into hyper-drive once you start digging into this book.

My own taste buds started tingling for rotisserie chicken in my early twenties when I was working as a chef in Toronto. On my days off I would explore the city's many ethnic neighborhoods, and in the Portuguese ones I found take-out shops selling the most divine rotisserie chicken. These businesses didn't need to advertise, because the alluring aroma of their chicken would literally pull customers off the street and into their stores. And once I saw their juicy, dripping-with-goodness chicken, I just had to have one.

When I didn't feel like cooking, picking up one of those chickens became an easy route to a tasty meal, and the leftovers were always welcome. I then began to try rotisserie chicken from other locations in Toronto; in Victoria, B.C., where I now live; and in whichever countries I traveled to, whether the United States, Singapore, France, or the Dominican Republic. No matter where I bought rotisserie chicken, each place had a different spin (pardon the pun!) on how to flavor the bird. I started to try and replicate some of them when cooking my own rotisserie chicken at home. Some of the results from that messing around in my kitchen can be found in this book.

I'm not alone in my love of this food. Although there has never been any shortage of people wanting to buy rotisserie chicken, it seems to have become even more popular in the past few years. We're all so busy but we still want to eat well, and many people feel that a rotisserie chicken is a quick, inexpensive, and crowd-pleasing way to satisfy that need.

Which explains why these chickens seem to be available everywhere you look these days, whether it's a food truck at a farmers' market, a fast-food or fine-dining restaurant, or a supermarket in any city. In 2013, according to estimates from the National Chicken Council, a trade association representing the U.S. chicken industry, 650 million rotisserie chickens were purchased from American supermarkets, club stores, and other food purveyors. Another 200 million were sold at food-service outlets. It's been estimated that Costco Wholesale alone sells 60 million of these chickens each year. And that's just in the United States. Rotisserie chicken is popular in Canada, Europe, and across Latin America too.

The truth is, we've been eating and enjoying rotisserie chicken since at least medieval times. The basics of cooking it have not changed a lot: put the bird on the spit, set it by the heat, rotate, and cook until done. What has changed, of course, is that electricity can now power the spit and make it go around, so there's no need to hand crank it. In many parts of the world, chickens are still cooked the old-fashioned way over coals; however, in this book you'll find information on how to turn your barbecue into a rotisserie as well as concise instructions on how to ready the chicken for the spit, techniques for cooking the bird if you don't have a barbecue or spit, and a step-by-step guide to carving the chicken once it's cooked.

Three recipe sections provide lots of options, whether you cook a chicken yourself, pick up one precooked, or use leftover chicken in other dishes. The first section offers ten ways to season chicken, inspired by flavors from around the world, such as Moroccan-spiced Chicken (page 24), Jerk Chicken (page 25), and Red Thai Curry Chicken (page 32).

Rotisserie chicken is also a fine ingredient to use in any recipe. To prove that fact, six chapters in the book's second section are dedicated to doing just that. Here are more than sixty recipes that incorporate rotisserie chicken meat, whether you cooked the bird yourself or bought it precooked from a supermarket. Hungry? Try appetizers, soups, salads, sandwiches, pasta dishes, and more, including Chili Chicken Mini Tostadas (page 50), Lentil and Chicken Soup with Herbes de Provence (page 67), Baby Kale Caesar Salad with Chicken (page 83), or Chicken Tikka Masala (page 141). Whether you have a whole chicken or leftover bits from a previous meal, there's a recipe to fit the bill.

Chicken pairs well with side dishes to create a quick and easy meal. Among the side salads, hot dishes, and breads in the third section are Sweet and Sour Coleslaw with Cranberries and Apricots (page 152), Garlic Mashed Potatoes with Kale (page 170), and Cheddar–Green Onion Wedge Biscuits (page 186).

At this point many of you are probably tying on your aprons, ready to start cooking a rotisserie chicken or trying new flavor combinations. If you weren't a rotisserie chicken lover before, you will be once you discover some of these recipes. So let's get cooking!

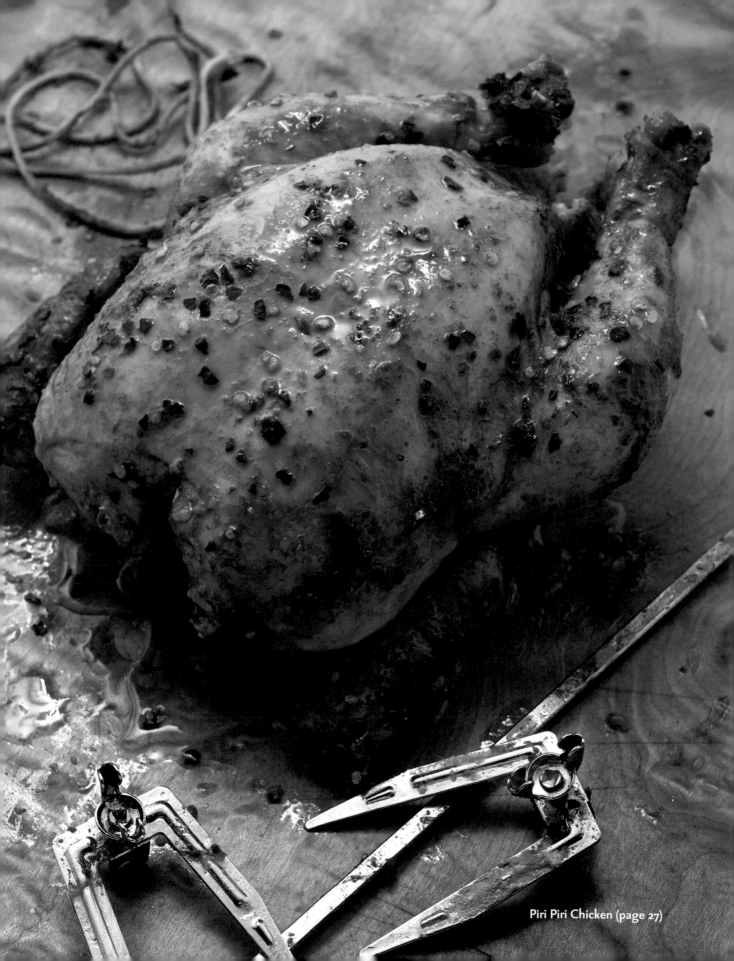

Piri Piri Chicken (page 27)

PREPARING YOUR ROTISSERIE CHICKEN AT HOME

Seasoning and Cooking Your Own Chicken

Red Thai Curry Chicken (page 32)

Rotisserie Chicken Basics

Choosing, Handling,
and Storing Fresh Whole Chicken

The recipes in this book that call for you to cook your own rotisserie chicken use a 3-pound (1.5 kg) bird. That size of chicken is classified as a fryer (see sidebar on pages 8–9), and it's the same type used by most stores that sell cooked, ready-to-eat rotisserie chicken. To me, it's perfect for the spit because this young chicken has tender meat, is always juicy, and cooks relatively quickly, ensuring you're not burdened with too long a wait before you can start eating. I have had success cooking all kinds of chicken, from standard, Grade A supermarket birds to pricier free-range ones bought from my local butcher. My advice is to let your budget, personal taste, and ethics dictate your choice.

When purchasing a whole chicken, choose a reputable store that sells lots of them and routinely brings in a fresh supply. In supermarkets, always check the best-before date on prepackaged chicken to ensure that what you're buying is fine for consumption. In places selling unpackaged chicken, such as a butcher shop displaying the birds in a showcase, don't be afraid to ask when the meat came in and when it should be used by.

You can also do your own visual check for freshness. The freshest uncooked chickens will look firm, have skin that tightly adheres to the body, and have rosy-pink flesh. If the bird feels soft, has sagging skin, and appears gray or pasty, it is not fresh and should not be purchased. To reduce the chance of spoilage, make the chicken the last thing you pick up at the store, and get it home and refrigerated as soon as you can.

Uncooked whole chicken can be stored for two to three days in the refrigerator before it is cooked. To ensure its juices won't drip on any foods, set the chicken in its original packaging in a shallow container and keep it in the lower part of the refrigerator until needed. Keep the chicken separate from other meats and produce, especially any foods that will be eaten raw. Once you unwrap the chicken, it should have a mild aroma. If it has a very strong, unpleasant odor that lingers, that's an indication the bird is not fresh. So is skin that feels filmy and overly sticky. If your chicken has these traits, don't eat it or you may risk getting food poisoning. Instead, throw it out, or if you're able to, return it in its original packaging to the store for a refund.

Any time you handle uncooked chicken, be sure to thoroughly wash your hands and any surfaces with which it will come into contact with soap and warm water. Do this both before and after handling raw chicken.

WHAT DO THESE TERMS MEAN?

Cornish chickens, originally from Britain, and White Rocks, developed in New England, are among the breeds of chicken that have been bred and crossbred commercially, which is why most retail food stores simply sell "chicken." You will, however, see chickens classified by size and grade and labeled according to how and where they were raised. Below is a summary of some of these terms.

AIR-CHILLED AND WATER-CHILLED: Chickens are cleaned before being packaged for sale, and this cleaning process can warm the meat. To prevent the chicken from deteriorating, it must then be quickly cooled using either refrigerated air or cold-water baths. Air chilling retains the chicken's natural flavor and color better than water chilling.

CERTIFIED ORGANIC: Governments and organic certification boards set specific standards that farmers must meet before they can sell their chicken as "organic." Although these rules can vary from nation to nation, in general the label "certified organic" guarantees that the chicken has been fed only certified organic feed that is free of animal by-products, antibiotics, and supplements. This process is more costly, as is the certification process, which is why organic chicken is more expensive than other types of chicken. Chickens labeled "organic" are also free-range, though the reverse is not necessarily true.

FREE-RANGE: This term means the chicken has had access to the outdoors, and this ability to move around and forage works the bird's muscles, literally building flavor. That combined with the more diverse diet, a mix of what the farmer feeds them plus what they are able to forage, is believed to enhance the flavor of the meat. Providing birds with space to move around outdoors requires a bigger area and more attention on the part of farmers, thus it is not suited to mass production. As a result, free-range chicken is more expensive to buy.

FREE-RUN: This term means the chicken has had the ability to move around freely within the barn. As with free-range chicken, this ability to move about is believed to enhance the bird's flavor. Providing this

Putting Together a Home Rotisserie

The best thing about rotisserie chicken, beyond its fabulous taste, is that you don't need a lot of equipment to cook your own. Many barbecues are built to accommodate a spit and its motor, and some models even come with these pieces included. If your barbecue is fitted for a spit and motor but didn't come with them, purchase these parts at a store that sells barbecues and accessories. Be sure to choose a version that fits your make and model of barbecue.

space means that fewer birds can be raised in a single barn, which makes free-run chicken more costly to produce than conventional chicken—and more costly at the store.

FRYER: A chicken less than ten weeks old that weighs between 2½ and 4½ pounds (1.25 and 2.0 kg). This young bird can be cooked by any method, including the rotisserie, which makes it the top seller at supermarkets.

GRADE A AND UTILITY: In many countries around the world, government inspectors visit processing plants to ensure that food safety standards are being met. They also grade meats and poultry according to certain standards. In Canada and the United States, the top grade is Grade A. Utility grade means the bird has cosmetic flaws, such as minor skin tears or other damage, which in no way affect the quality of the meat but will make the bird look less appealing when cooked.

GRAIN-FED AND VEGETARIAN GRAIN-FED: All commercially raised chickens are fed grain, but some producers highlight this fact on the label by using the term "grain fed." Vegetarian grain-fed means that the feed contains no animal by-products, such as bone meal, which are sometimes added to feed as a protein source.

HALAL AND KOSHER: In Arabic, the word *halal* means "permitted or lawful." Halal chicken has been bred and processed in a way that meets Islamic dietary guidelines. Kosher chicken has been processed to conform to Jewish dietary laws.

NATURAL: This term means the chicken contains no artificial ingredients, coloring, or chemical preservatives and has not been brined, rubbed, flavored, or enhanced in any way for cooking.

ROASTER OR ROASTING CHICKEN: A young chicken between eight and twelve weeks old that weighs 5 pounds (2.3 kg) or more. That size makes it great for roasting.

The spit is simply a sturdy—often stainless-steel—metal rod. It comes fitted with adjustable metal prongs that slide onto the rod to hold the chicken or other food in place. The motor is a not overly large device that clips onto the side of the barbecue with a slot that you slide and secure the spit into. Choose a heavy-duty motor if you plan to use your rotisserie a lot or cook more than one chicken on it. Some of the motors are electric and need to be plugged in. Before choosing this type, be sure you have an outdoor power source near your barbecue. If you don't, purchase a battery-powered or solar-powered motor.

Other items you'll need to prepare the chicken are a heat-proof pan to set under the chicken as it cooks. A disposable foil pan will work, but I prefer to designate a metal or cast-iron pan for use on the barbecue. You'll also require an apron to keep you tidy, butcher's twine to truss the chicken, a barbecue brush for basting, a timer to keep track of how long the chicken has been cooking, an instant-read thermometer to tell you when it's cooked, and insulated barbecue mitts to pull the spit off the barbecue when the chicken is cooked.

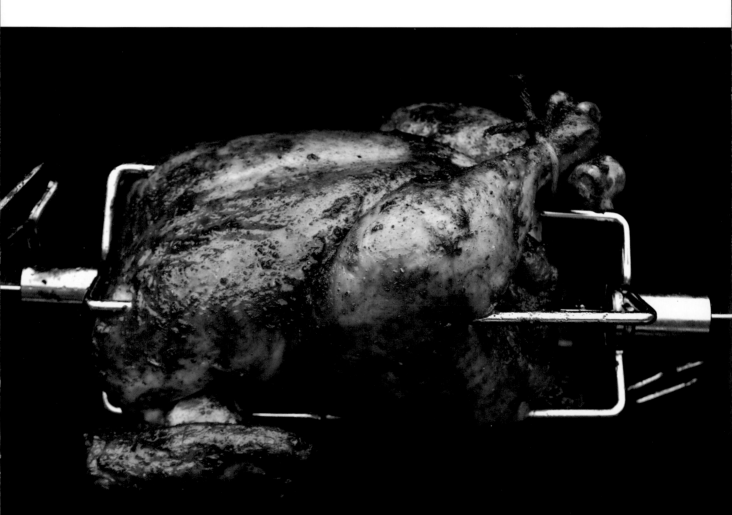

Preparing Chicken for the Spit

Raw chicken can harbor harmful bacteria that may cause food poisoning, so be sure to practice proper food safety. Below are some guidelines.

- Thoroughly wash your hands with soap and warm water both before and after handling raw chicken.
- Thoroughly clean your work space and the equipment you'll be using with hot and soapy water, before you start preparing the chicken.
- Avoid rinsing your chicken with cold water before using it. Doing this can splatter and spread bacteria around your kitchen and dilute the flavor of the meat; proper cooking will kill any bacteria on the meat itself.
- Dedicate a cutting board for raw foods such as chicken, and another for vegetables and cooked foods.
- Keep the chicken refrigerated at all times when you are not working with it.
- Thoroughly clean everything that comes in contact with your hands and the chicken, such as cutting boards, counters, kitchen towels, utensils, and faucets.

Trussing the Chicken

Before cooking a chicken on a rotisserie, you need to truss the bird. Do this by neatly tying it with kitchen twine so the chicken's legs and wings stay in place as it goes around on the spit. Trussing also ensures the chicken cooks more evenly. Below are step-by-step information and photos on how to truss.

1. If the skin of the bird is moist from the way it was packaged, pat it dry with paper towel before trussing. Stuff the chicken with flavorings, if that is part of your recipe. Cut a piece of kitchen twine to a length of 5 feet (1.5 m). Set the chicken on a clean work surface, breast side up. Now fold and tuck the wings under the chicken's body. With the breast side up, draw the twine around the tail, cross it over, and then take it around the end of each drumstick.
2. Draw the twine up tightly between the drumsticks and thighs.
3. Extend the twine around the outside of each leg and over the wings.
4. Turn the bird over, so it is breast side down. Take each end of twine over the folded wings and shoulders of the bird.
5. Pull the twine tightly and tie a knot to secure it in place. Use scissors to cut away excess string. The chicken is now ready for seasoning and cooking.

HOW CAN I FLAVOR ROTISSERIE CHICKEN?

Herbs and spices are often used to impart the skin and meat of the chicken with additional flavor as it cooks. Here are a few of the most common ways to apply these and other flavoring ingredients.

WET MARINADES: A mix of liquids and seasonings, often containing an acidic ingredient such as lemon juice, that is used to coat and infuse the chicken with flavor.

RUBS: A mix of dry spices and herbs that is worked into the skin and meat using your hands.

BRINES: In its most basic form, a solution of salt dissolved in water. Other ingredients, such as sweeteners, spices, herbs, fruit juices, or alcohol, are sometimes added. The chicken is then soaked in the brine to allow the flavors and the moisture to permeate it.

For rotisserie chicken, I prefer rubs and marinades. I consider brines to be a good choice for lean cuts of meats and those that require long, slow cooking and might dry out. However, as a rotisserie chicken spins around on the spit, there is ample fat in its flesh and skin to keep it moist during cooking. And since it is not cooking for hours and hours, there's no chance it will dry out. Plus, I find that brines can impart a noticeable salty taste, which I find interferes with the natural, give-me-more flavor of a good chicken.

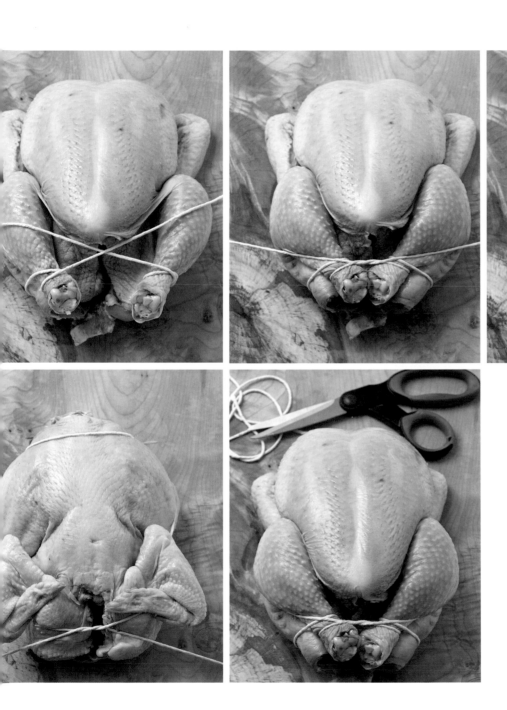

Cooking and Resting the Bird

Before you start cooking the chicken, ensure your barbecue is properly preheated to the temperature indicated in the recipe. Putting the chicken on before the barbecue is preheated will throw off the cooking time, and your chicken may not cook evenly. After sliding the chicken onto the spit, ensure the prongs that hold it in place are securely anchored into the meat. If not, the chicken will slip off the prongs and not spin around on the spit.

During cooking, keep the barbecue at a constant temperature as outlined in the recipe. If the temperature fluctuates too much, it will throw off your cooking time and cause the bird to cook unevenly, or even scorch if the heat goes too high.

Although cooking times are given in each recipe, the best way to gauge doneness is to use an instant-read thermometer. To test for doneness, turn off the spit and insert the thermometer into the deepest part of the thigh, not touching the bone; if it registers 170°F (77°C), the chicken is cooked. Remove the chicken from the spit, set it on a plate, loosely tent it with aluminum foil, and allow it to rest for at least 10 minutes. The resting process allows the juices to set, ensuring that most of them remain in the chicken after it is carved.

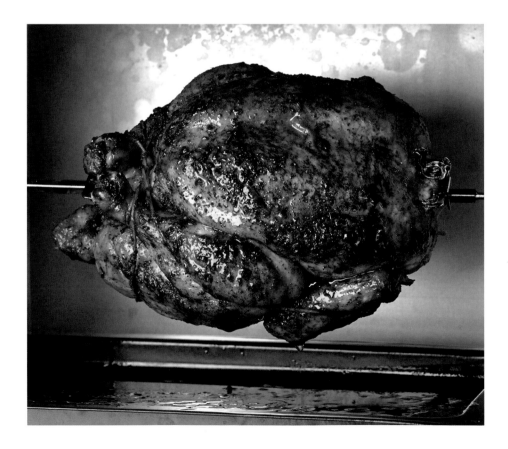

If you don't have a barbecue fitted with a spit on which to cook the rotisserie chicken recipes, here are three other methods you can use. Always transfer cooked chicken to a plate, loosely tent it with aluminum foil, and allow it to rest for at least 10 minutes before carving and serving.

SKILLET ON THE BARBECUE: If you have a barbecue but no rotisserie spit, cook the chicken in a skillet on the barbecue. It won't have that all-around rich color a rotisserie chicken has, but it will still attain a pleasing smoky flavor.

To cook it, preheat your barbecue to 400°F (200°C). After trussing and flavoring the chicken, set it in a cast-iron skillet or another pan suitable for the barbecue. Set the skillet on one side of the barbecue, close the lid, and turn the heat off underneath the chicken but leave the other side of the barbecue on. Cook the chicken, brushing it occasionally with the pan juices, for 75 to 90 minutes, or until an instant-read thermometer inserted into the deepest part of the thigh, not touching the bone, registers 170°F (77°C). Check the temperature as the chicken cooks, and adjust the flame as needed to maintain a constant temperature of 400°F (200°C).

TABLETOP ROTISSERIE OVEN: If you live in a small space or prefer the ease of a smaller unit, a tabletop rotisserie oven will allow you to cook the chicken inside with great results. Most ovens will accommodate a chicken up to 5 pounds (2.3 kg), which is suitable for the rotisserie recipes in this book.

To cook the chicken, preheat the oven to 375°F (190°C). While the oven heats up, slide the chicken onto the oven's rotisserie spit and secure it. Set a heat-proof pan under the chicken to catch the tasty juices seeping from the bird. Add a little water to the pan so the first drips don't scorch it. Turn your rotisserie motor on. Cook the chicken, brushing it occasionally with the pan juices, for 75 to 90 minutes, or until an instant-read thermometer inserted into the deepest part of the thigh, not touching the bone, registers 170°F (77°C).

CONVENTIONAL OVEN: If you don't have a barbecue or a rotisserie oven with a spit, you could also simply cook the chicken in a regular oven. As with cooking the chicken in a skillet on the barbecue, it won't have that all-around rich color a rotisserie chicken has, but it will still be juicy and tasty.

To cook the chicken, preheat the oven to 375°F (190°C). After trussing and flavoring the chicken, set it in a shallow-sided roasting pan. Roast the chicken, brushing it occasionally with the pan juices, for 90 minutes, or until an instant-read thermometer inserted into the deepest part of the thigh, not touching the bone, registers 170°F (77°C).

Carving the Chicken

Learning to carve a chicken into nice, neat pieces will make it present better and ensure everyone gets a portion of white and dark meat. Below is step-by-step information on how to carve the bird into twelve perfect pieces. The photos will guide you on exactly where to place the knife before cutting.

1. Set the whole chicken on a cutting board, breast side up. Bend a leg away from the body until the thigh bone unhinges from the body. Now use a sharp, thin-bladed carving knife to remove the leg from the body, cutting through the separated joint. Repeat this step to remove the other leg.

2. Cut through the joint and separate each leg into drumstick and thigh pieces and set them on a serving platter.

3. Starting at the tail end, begin by removing one side of the breast from the body by cutting along the breastbone with the tip of your knife. When you reach the wishbone, situated just above the wing, cut down along the wishbone toward the wing and remove the breast meat. Repeat this cut on the other side of the chicken.

4. Cut each breast, widthwise, into two pieces and set them on a platter.

5. Cut each wing off the carcass by slicing through the joint that connects the wing to the lower part of the breast. Split each wing into two pieces, cutting between the drumette, the part of the wing that was attached to the breast, and the wingette, the middle portion of the wing. Set the wing pieces on the platter, and the chicken is ready to serve. Save the chicken carcass to make chicken stock (see page 59).

TEN WAYS TO FLAVOR ROTISSERIE CHICKEN

Traditional Barbecued Rotisserie Chicken . . . 20

Spanish-style Chicken . . . 23

Moroccan-spiced Chicken . . . 24

Jerk Chicken . . . 25

Piri Piri Chicken . . . 27

Maple-Mustard Chicken with Coriander and Pepper . . . 28

Chinese-style Barbecue Chicken . . . 29

Tandoori Chicken . . . 30

Red Thai Curry Chicken . . . 32

Sunday Dinner Rotisserie Chicken . . . 33

Traditional Barbecued Rotisserie Chicken

This juicy orangey red–hued chicken looks similar to the barbecue-spiced rotisserie chickens sold at most supermarkets. Its flavor, though, is more complex and intriguing thanks to the splendid and aromatic spice rub you make yourself. Feel free to experiment with the ingredients in the rub; for example, if you like its smoky taste, use smoked paprika instead of the regular (sweet) paprika used in this recipe. Like things spicy? Double the amount of cayenne. This rub recipe makes ⅔ cup (160 mL), which is more than you need for one 3-pound (1.5 kg) chicken, but it keeps well in an airtight container.

Prep time: 20 minutes • Cooking time: 75 to 90 minutes • Makes: 4 servings

Traditional rub

¼ cup (60 mL) chili powder

3 Tbsp (45 mL) ground cumin

1 Tbsp (15 mL) ground oregano

1 Tbsp (15 mL) paprika

1 Tbsp (15 mL) sea or kosher salt

2 tsp (10 mL) ground sage

2 tsp (10 mL) freshly ground black pepper

1 tsp (5 mL) onion powder

½ tsp (2 mL) garlic powder

¼ tsp (1 mL) cayenne pepper

Traditional barbecued chicken

1 medium onion, quartered

2 large garlic cloves, sliced

1 whole chicken, 3 lb/1.5 kg

4 tsp (20 mL) olive oil

3 to 4 tsp (15 to 20 mL) Traditional Rub (see above), or to taste

Traditional rub

1. Combine all ingredients in a bowl until well mixed, then transfer to an airtight container and store at room temperature. This rub will keep up to 6 months.

Traditional barbecued chicken

1. Stuff the onions and garlic into the cavity of the chicken, then truss it and set it on a wide plate (see Preparing Chicken for the Spit, page 11).

2. Brush and coat the outside of the chicken with the olive oil. Sprinkle the bird with the rub and, using your hands, rub it into the skin, ensuring it reaches deep into the areas between the breasts and legs and the tucked parts of each wing.

3. Preheat the barbecue to 400°F (200°C). While the barbecue heats up, slide the chicken onto one end of the rotisserie spit and secure it.

4. Place the spit on the barbecue and set a heat-proof pan under the chicken to catch the tasty juices seeping from the bird. Add a little water to the pan so the first drips don't scorch it. Turn the rotisserie motor on.

5. Close the lid on the barbecue and turn off the heat directly under the chicken. Leave the other side of the barbecue between medium and medium-high. Cook the chicken, brushing it occasionally with the pan juices, for 75 to 90 minutes, or until an instant-read thermometer inserted into the deepest part of the thigh, not touching the bone, registers 170°F (77°C). As the chicken cooks, adjust the flame as needed to maintain a constant temperature of 400°F (200°C).

6. Remove the chicken from the spit, set it on a plate, loosely tent it with aluminum foil, and allow it to rest for 10 minutes before carving and serving. See Carving the Chicken (page 16).

Note: If you don't have a barbecue with a spit, or you don't have a barbecue at all, on page 15 you'll find three alternative ways to cook the chicken.

Spanish-style Chicken

This chicken is flavored with a mix of olive oil, lemon, spices, and herbs. Serve it on your patio with a cool glass of Spanish rosé wine, side dishes of Pesto-roasted Red Potatoes (page 169) and Grilled Zucchini with Pine Nuts and Parmesan (page 167), and say Olé!

Prep time: 15 minutes, plus marinating time • Cooking time: 75 to 90 minutes • Makes: 4 servings

3 Tbsp (45 mL) olive oil + more for
  drizzling
2 tsp (10 mL) finely grated lemon zest
2 Tbsp (30 mL) lemon juice + more for
  drizzling
1 large garlic clove, minced
1 tsp (5 mL) dried oregano
1 tsp (5 mL) paprika
1 tsp (5 mL) ground cumin
¼ tsp (1 mL) cayenne pepper
1 whole chicken, 3 lb/1.5 kg
Salt and freshly ground black pepper
  to taste

1. In a small bowl, combine the olive oil, lemon zest and juice, garlic, oregano, paprika, cumin, and cayenne. Set aside.

2. Truss the chicken and set it in a shallow-sided glass or ceramic dish (see Preparing Chicken for the Spit, page 11). Brush and coat the outside of the chicken with the marinade, ensuring it reaches deep into the areas between the breasts and legs and the tucked parts of each wing. Cover the chicken with plastic wrap and refrigerate for 4 hours, turning the bird occasionally.

3. When ready to cook, let the chicken sit at room temperature for 30 minutes to take the chill from the meat and allow it to cook more evenly on the spit.

4. Preheat the barbecue to 400°F (200°C). While the barbecue heats up, season the chicken with salt and pepper, then slide it onto one end of the rotisserie spit and secure it. Brush the chicken with any leftover marinade, then cook, baste, and allow it to rest, as per the Traditional Barbecued Rotisserie Chicken (page 20).

5. Carve the chicken and set it on a serving platter (see Carving the Chicken, page 16). Serve drizzled with a little olive oil and lemon juice for added richness and tang.

Moroccan-spiced Chicken

When you blend the citrus juice and zest, mint, garlic, cumin, and other spices used in the marinade for this chicken, you get an instant and aromatic sense of what Moroccan cuisine is all about: flavor, flavor, flavor! Try serving it with couscous and Orange, Avocado, and Red Onion Salad (page 153).

Prep time: 20 minutes, plus marinating time • Cooking time: 75 to 90 minutes • Makes: 4 servings

3 Tbsp (45 mL) olive oil

1 tsp (5 mL) finely grated lemon zest

1 Tbsp (15 mL) lemon juice

1 tsp (5 mL) finely grated orange zest

1 Tbsp (15 mL) orange juice

¼ cup (60 mL) chopped fresh mint leaves

1 large garlic clove, minced

2 tsp (10 mL) ground cumin

1 tsp (5 mL) paprika

½ tsp (2 mL) ground coriander

¼ tsp (1 mL) cayenne pepper

1 whole chicken, 3 lb/1.5 kg

Salt and freshly ground black pepper
   to taste

1. In a small bowl, combine the olive oil, lemon zest and juice, orange zest and juice, mint, garlic, cumin, paprika, coriander, and cayenne. Set aside.

2. Truss the chicken and set it in a shallow-sided glass or ceramic dish (see Preparing Chicken for the Spit, page 11). Brush and coat the outside of the chicken with the marinade, ensuring it reaches deep into the areas between the breasts and legs and the tucked parts of each wing. Cover the chicken with plastic wrap and refrigerate for 4 hours, turning the bird occasionally.

3. When ready to cook, let the chicken sit at room temperature for 30 minutes to take the chill from the meat and allow it to cook more evenly on the spit.

4. Preheat the barbecue to 400°F (200°C). While the barbecue heats up, season the chicken with salt and pepper, then slide it on one end of the rotisserie spit and secure it. Brush the chicken with any leftover marinade, then cook, baste, and allow it to rest, as per the Traditional Barbecued Rotisserie Chicken (page 20).

5. Carve the chicken and set it on a serving platter (see Carving the Chicken, page 16).

Jerk Chicken

In Jamaica, jerk dishes are very popular, and each cook has their own seasoning recipe. Chilies, onions, garlic, thyme, and spices, such as nutmeg and allspice, are common to most. Wear rubber gloves when chopping and handling the fiery hot pepper in this recipe, and be careful not to put your fingers near your eyes or skin.

Prep time: 20 minutes, plus marinating time • Cooking time: 75 to 90 minutes • Makes: 4 servings

1 Scotch bonnet, habanero, or serrano pepper, seeded and coarsely chopped, or 1 tsp (5 mL) dried, crushed chili flakes

¼ cup (60 mL) finely chopped fresh cilantro

2 green onions, very thinly sliced

1 large garlic clove, minced

1 tsp (5 mL) ground allspice

¼ tsp (1 mL) ground nutmeg

2 Tbsp (30 mL) lime juice

1 Tbsp (15 mL) cider vinegar

1 Tbsp (15 mL) brown sugar

1 Tbsp (15 mL) vegetable oil

1 whole chicken, 3 lb/1.5 kg

Salt and freshly ground black pepper to taste

1. In a small bowl, combine the peppers, cilantro, green onions, garlic, allspice, nutmeg, lime juice, vinegar, sugar, and vegetable oil. Set aside.

2. Truss the chicken and set it in a shallow-sided glass or ceramic dish (see Preparing Chicken for the Spit, page 11). Brush and coat the outside of the chicken with the jerk mixture, ensuring it reaches deep into the areas between the breasts and legs and the tucked parts of each wing. Cover the chicken with plastic wrap and refrigerate for 4 hours, turning the bird occasionally.

3. When ready to cook, let the chicken sit at room temperature for 30 minutes to take the chill from the meat and allow it to cook more evenly on the spit.

4. Preheat the barbecue to 400°F (200°C). While the barbecue heats up, season the chicken with salt and pepper, then slide it onto one end of the rotisserie spit and secure it. Brush the chicken with any leftover jerk mixture, then cook, baste, and allow it to rest, as per the Traditional Barbecued Rotisserie Chicken (page 20).

5. Carve the chicken and set it on a serving platter (see Carving the Chicken, page 16).

ABOUT JERK

Spanish explorers to Jamaica discovered that the island's Arawak Indians used generous amounts of spices and peppers to help preserve dried meats. In Spanish, the word for dried meat is *charqui*, which is said to have inspired the English words "jerk" and "jerky." Today jerk has come to mean a seasoning for foods such as chicken, rather than a preservative.

Piri Piri Chicken

Piri piri is the Swahili term for the spicy bird's-eye chili used in Africa. During colonial times, Portuguese inhabitants used these chilies to make a hot sauce they called—you guessed it—piri piri. At the time, it was used to flavor flame-cooked foods such as chicken, and it still is. This version of piri piri chicken uses fresh serrano chilies or crushed chili flakes, which are easier to find. After cooking, the carved chicken is generously drizzled with a lemony butter mixture.

Prep time: 20 minutes, plus marinating time • Cooking time: 75 to 90 minutes • Makes: 4 servings

3 Tbsp (45 mL) olive oil

2 tsp (10 mL) finely grated lemon zest

3 Tbsp (45 mL) lemon juice, divided

2 large garlic cloves, minced

1½ tsp (7 mL) dried, crushed chili flakes or 1 or 2 small finely chopped fresh serrano chilies

1 tsp (5 mL) ground oregano

1 tsp (5 mL) paprika

1 whole chicken, 3 lb/1.5 kg

Salt and freshly ground black pepper to taste

2 Tbsp (30 mL) butter

1 tsp (5 mL) hot pepper sauce

2 Tbsp (30 mL) chopped fresh cilantro, mint, or parsley

8 lemon slices, for garnish

1. In a small bowl, combine the olive oil, lemon zest, 2 Tbsp (30 mL) of the lemon juice, the garlic, chili flakes (or chopped chilies), oregano, and paprika. Set aside.

2. Truss the chicken and set it in a shallow-sided glass or ceramic dish (see Preparing Chicken for the Spit, page 11). Brush and coat the outside of the chicken with the marinade, ensuring it reaches deep into the areas between the breasts and legs and the tucked parts of each wing. Cover the chicken with plastic wrap and refrigerate for 4 hours, turning the bird occasionally.

3. When ready to cook, let the chicken sit at room temperature for 30 minutes to take the chill from the meat and allow it to cook more evenly on the spit.

4. Preheat the barbecue to 400°F (200°C). While the barbecue heats up, season the chicken with salt and pepper, then slide it onto one end of the rotisserie spit and secure it. Brush the chicken with any leftover marinade, then cook, baste, and allow it to rest, as per the Traditional Barbecued Rotisserie Chicken (page 20).

5. Place the butter, 1 Tbsp (15 mL) of lemon juice, the hot pepper sauce, and the cilantro (mint or parsley) in a very small pot. Set over medium heat and cook just until the butter is melted. Remove from the heat.

6. Carve the chicken and set it on a serving platter (see Carving the Chicken, page 16). Drizzle with the butter mixture, garnish with lemon slices, and serve.

Maple-Mustard Chicken with Coriander and Pepper

Globally inspired, this inviting chicken dish features sweet Canadian maple syrup, pungent French mustard, and aromatic Indian coriander seeds. The flavoring is an appealing combination of ingredients that are readily at hand in my kitchen—and quite possibly in yours too.

Prep time: 20 minutes, plus marinating time • Cooking time: 75 to 90 minutes • Makes: 4 servings

2 Tbsp (30 mL) maple syrup or honey

2 Tbsp (30 mL) smooth or whole-grain Dijon mustard

1 tsp (5 mL) finely grated lime zest

1 Tbsp (15 mL) lime juice

1 tsp (5 mL) ground coriander seeds

1 tsp (5 mL) coarsely cracked black peppercorns (see Note)

½ tsp (2 mL) paprika

⅛ tsp (0.5 mL) cayenne pepper

1 whole chicken, 3 lb/1.5 kg

Salt to taste

Note: To coarsely crack black peppercorns, use the coarsest setting on your pepper grinder. You can also set the whole peppercorns on a cutting board, place a heavy skillet over them, and roll it back and forth while applying pressure to crack them.

1. In a small bowl, combine the maple syrup (or honey), mustard, lime zest and juice, coriander seeds, peppercorns, paprika, and cayenne. Set aside.

2. Truss the chicken and set it in a shallow-sided glass or ceramic dish (see Preparing Chicken for the Spit, page 11). Brush and coat the outside of the chicken with the marinade, ensuring it reaches deep into the areas between the breasts and legs and the tucked parts of each wing. Cover the chicken with plastic wrap and refrigerate for 4 hours, turning the bird occasionally.

3. When ready to cook, let the chicken sit at room temperature for 30 minutes to take the chill from the meat and allow it to cook more evenly on the spit.

4. Preheat the barbecue to 400°F (200°C). While the barbecue heats up, season the chicken with salt, then slide it onto one end of the rotisserie spit and secure it. Brush the chicken with any leftover marinade, then cook, baste, and allow it to rest, as per the Traditional Barbecued Rotisserie Chicken (page 20).

5. Carve the chicken and set it on a serving platter (see Carving the Chicken, page 16).

Chinese-style Barbecue Chicken

This sumptuous, lacquered-looking chicken is flavored in a similar fashion to the barbecued meats you'll see for sale in your local Chinatown. The marinade is a hybrid of several recipes found in my collection of Chinese cookbooks. Make a nice meal by serving the chicken with steamed rice and Vegetable Chop Suey with Cashews (page 172).

Prep time: 20 minutes, plus marinating time • Cooking time: 75 to 90 minutes • Makes: 4 servings

2 Tbsp (30 mL) soy sauce

2 Tbsp (30 mL) ketchup

1 Tbsp (15 mL) dry sherry, brandy, or
　Chinese cooking wine

1 Tbsp (15 mL) honey

2 tsp (10 mL) grated fresh ginger

1 large garlic clove, minced

½ tsp (2 mL) five-spice powder

Salt and freshly ground black pepper
　to taste

1 whole chicken, 3 lb/1.5 kg

Sliced green onions, for garnish
　(optional)

Toasted sesame seeds, for garnish
　(optional)

1. In a small bowl, combine the soy sauce, ketchup, sherry (brandy or wine), honey, ginger, garlic, five-spice powder, and pepper. Set aside.

2. Truss the chicken and set it in a shallow-sided glass or ceramic dish (see Preparing Chicken for the Spit, page 11). Brush and coat the outside of the chicken with the marinade, ensuring it reaches deep into the areas between the breasts and legs and the tucked parts of each wing. Cover the chicken with plastic wrap and refrigerate for 4 hours, turning the bird occasionally.

3. When ready to cook, let the chicken sit at room temperature for 30 minutes to take the chill from the meat and allow it to cook more evenly on the spit.

4. Preheat the barbecue to 400°F (200°C). While the barbecue heats up, season the chicken with salt, then slide it onto one end of the rotisserie spit and secure it. Brush the chicken with any leftover marinade, then cook, baste, and allow it to rest, as per the Traditional Barbecued Rotisserie Chicken (page 20).

5. Carve the chicken and set it on a serving platter (see Carving the Chicken, page 16). For added texture and flavor, sprinkle the carved chicken with sliced green onions and toasted sesame seeds.

Tandoori Chicken

In traditional Indian restaurants, tandoori chicken is cooked in a tandoor, a clay or metal oven. In this recipe, the cooking is done on the barbecue and the results are equally delicious. Tandoori paste, available in the Asian food aisle of many supermarkets, colors the bird a beguiling pinkish-red. It contains ingredients such as ginger, tamarind, garlic powder, coriander, and cumin. It also contains salt, which is why none is added in this recipe.

Prep time: 10 minutes, plus marinating time • Cooking time: 75 to 90 minutes • Makes: 4 servings

⅓ cup (80 mL) tandoori paste

2 Tbsp (30 mL) plain thick yogurt, such as Greek-style

1 Tbsp (15 mL) lime juice

1 whole chicken, 3 lb/1.5 kg

Chopped fresh mint or cilantro, for garnish (optional)

1. In a small bowl, combine the tandoori paste, yogurt, and lime juice. Set aside.

2. Truss the chicken and set it in a shallow-sided glass or ceramic dish (see Preparing Chicken for the Spit, page 11). Brush and coat the outside of the chicken with the tandoori mixture, ensuring it reaches deep into the areas between the breasts and legs and the tucked parts of each wing. Cover the chicken with plastic wrap and refrigerate for 4 hours, turning the bird occasionally.

3. When ready to cook, let the chicken sit at room temperature for 30 minutes to take the chill from the meat and allow it to cook more evenly on the spit.

4. Preheat the barbecue to 400°F (200°C). While the barbecue heats up, slide the chicken onto one end of the rotisserie spit and secure it. Brush the chicken with any leftover marinade, then cook, baste, and allow it to rest, as per the Traditional Barbecued Rotisserie Chicken (page 20).

5. Carve the chicken and set it on a serving platter (see Carving the Chicken, page 16). For added flavor and color, sprinkle the carved chicken with chopped fresh mint or cilantro.

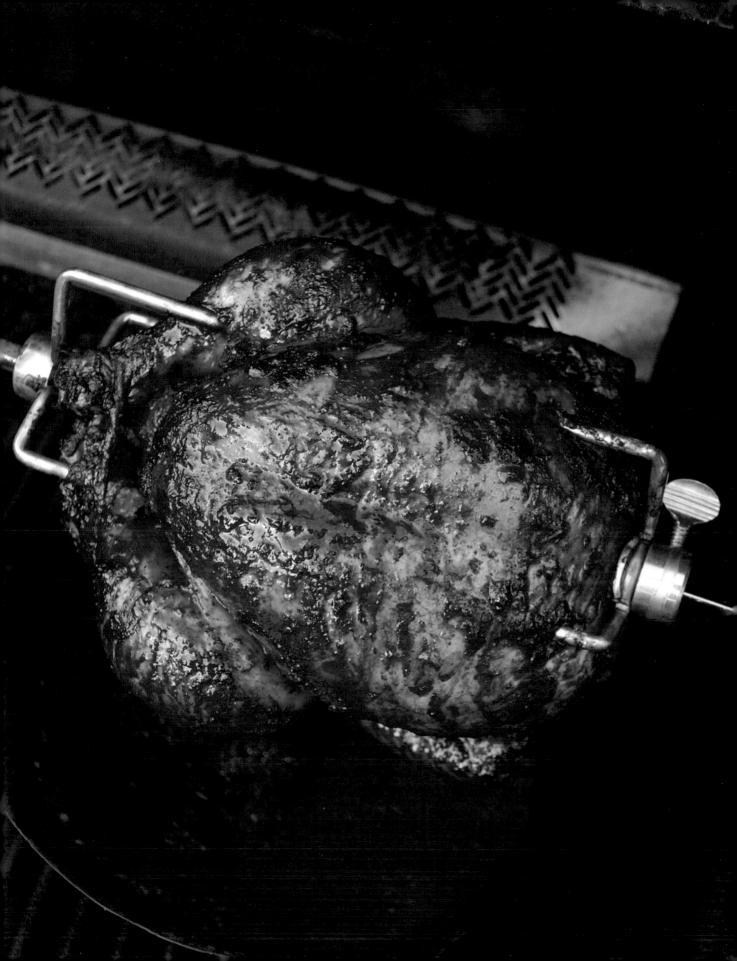

Red Thai Curry Chicken

Thai-style curry pastes come in three colors: red, green, and yellow. The type of hot chili and other seasonings, such as garlic, spices, and herbs, determine the color. In this recipe, I've used a modest amount of red curry paste to spice up rotisserie chicken. If you like "the heat," you could, of course, add more. Look for curry pastes in the Asian food aisle of your grocery store.

Prep time: 20 minutes, plus marinating time • Cooking time: 75 to 90 minutes • Makes: 4 servings

2 Tbsp (30 mL) orange juice

1 Tbsp (15 mL) lime juice

1 Tbsp (15 mL) vegetable oil

1 Tbsp (15 mL) soy sauce

1½ tsp (7 mL) honey

1 Tbsp (15 mL) Thai red curry paste

2 tsp (10 mL) freshly grated ginger

¼ cup (60 mL) chopped fresh mint or cilantro

1 whole chicken, 3 lb/1.5 kg

Salt and freshly ground black pepper to taste

1. In a small bowl, combine the orange and lime juices, vegetable oil, soy sauce, honey, curry paste, ginger, and mint (or cilantro). Set aside.

2. Truss the chicken and set it in a shallow-sided glass or ceramic dish (see Preparing Chicken for the Spit, page 11). Brush and coat the outside of the chicken with the curry mixture, ensuring it reaches deep into the areas between the breasts and legs and the tucked parts of each wing. Cover the chicken with plastic wrap and refrigerate for 4 hours, turning the bird occasionally.

3. When ready to cook, let the chicken sit at room temperature for 30 minutes to take the chill from the meat and allow it to cook more evenly on the spit.

4. Preheat the barbecue to 400°F (200°C). While the barbecue heats up, season the chicken with salt and pepper, then slide it onto one end of the rotisserie spit and secure it. Brush the chicken with any leftover marinade, then cook, baste, and allow it to rest, as per the Traditional Barbecued Rotisserie Chicken (page 20).

5. Carve the chicken and set it on a serving platter (see Carving the Chicken, page 16).

Sunday Dinner Rotisserie Chicken

My wife and I often eat roast chicken for Sunday dinner, and we flavor it with such things as lemon, garlic, and sage. One hot summer's day, we had a craving for that chicken but didn't want to cook it inside. So, outside I went and cooked the bird on my rotisserie, and the result was as delicious as roasting it in the oven—maybe even more so.

Prep time: 20 minutes, plus marinating time • Cooking time: 75 to 90 minutes • Makes: 4 servings

1 large lemon + another ½ lemon for drizzling

3 Tbsp (45 mL) olive oil + more for drizzling

2 Tbsp (30 mL) chopped fresh sage

1 whole chicken, 3 lb/1.5 kg

8 garlic cloves, thinly sliced

1 large onion, cut in 8 wedges

8 whole fresh sage leaves

Salt and freshly ground black pepper to taste

1. Finely zest the whole lemon into a shallow-sided glass or ceramic dish large enough to hold the chicken. Cut that lemon in half and squeeze the juice into the dish with the zest. Stir in the olive oil and chopped sage. Cut the juiced lemon into chunks and set aside.

2. With your fingers, carefully lift up the skin off the top of each breast and slide half of the garlic slices underneath, pushing the pieces into different spots around the chicken.

3. Stuff the onion wedges, lemon chunks, remaining garlic, and whole sage leaves into the cavity of the chicken. Truss the chicken (see Preparing Chicken for the Spit, page 11).

4. Set the chicken in the dish containing the marinade. Brush and coat the outside of the chicken with the marinade, ensuring it reaches deep into the areas between the breasts and legs and the tucked parts of each wing. Cover the chicken with plastic wrap and refrigerate for 4 hours, turning the bird occasionally.

5. When ready to cook, let the chicken sit at room temperature for 30 minutes to take the chill from the meat and allow it to cook more evenly on the spit.

6. Preheat the barbecue to 400°F (200°C). While the barbecue heats up, season the chicken with salt and pepper, then slide it onto one end of the rotisserie spit and secure it. Brush the chicken with any leftover marinade, then cook, baste, and allow it to rest, as per the Traditional Barbecued Rotisserie Chicken (page 20).

7. Carve the chicken and set it on a serving platter (see Carving the Chicken, page 16). Serve drizzled with a little olive oil and lemon juice for added richness and tang.

Teriyaki Chicken Stir-fry with Orange and Ginger (page 138)

COOKING WITH YOUR ROTISSERIE CHICKEN

Recipes Made with Your Storebought or Homecooked Chicken

Rotisserie Chicken for Recipes

Buying, Storing, and Handling Cooked Rotisserie Chicken

Storebought rotisserie chicken is a wonderful thing, but it's important to follow good food-safe practices when buying and handling it. Government health agencies advise that bacteria can multiply rapidly on poultry and reach dangerous levels in the temperature range between 40°F (4°C) and 140°F (60°C). To ensure your hot rotisserie chicken is not in that range for long, make it the last item you pick up in the grocery store and take it straight home. Be sure the chicken you buy has been stored in a hot case at a food-safe temperature above 140°F (60°C). When in doubt, check with the store manager or simply don't buy it. And make sure you purchase precooked chickens from places that sell lots of them, so you know they're being freshly cooked rather than sitting around steaming and losing flavor.

Eat or refrigerate your rotisserie chicken within two hours of purchase—or within two hours of cooking your own chicken. On a hot day, use or refrigerate it within an hour of purchase or cooking. You can store leftover chicken in an airtight container and refrigerate it for up to three days. If you're not able to use it within that time, freeze it. Simply slice, shred, or cube cold chicken leftovers, place them in an airtight container, label and date it, then freeze for up to three months.

Whether you cook your own chicken or buy it precooked, here's a guide to cutting and preparing it for use in the following recipes.

Preparing Carved Pieces

These cooked pieces of leg, wing, and/or breast are simply cut from the chicken and incorporated into a recipe. To learn how to cut the chicken, see Carving the Chicken (page 16).

If your whole rotisserie chicken is cold because you bought it that way, or because the one you purchased has cooled, you can reheat it if needed. Preheat the oven to 300°F (150°C) and line a baking sheet with parchment paper. Carve the bird into pieces, set them on the baking sheet, and place them in the oven for 20 to 25 minutes or so, until they are hot again. Use as described in the recipe.

Creating Sliced, Diced, or Shredded Pieces

These pieces have been removed from the bone and cut or pulled into pieces. Simply slice the meat into thin pieces suitable for what you're making, or into the size of cubes called for in the recipe. Diced means you cut the meat in ½-inch (1.25 cm) cubes. Finely diced means you cut it into ¼-inch (6 mm) or even smaller cubes. In recipes calling for shredded chicken, the cooked meat, unless otherwise indicated, is pulled into pieces about ½ inch (1.25 cm) wide and 2 to 3 inches (5 to 7.5 cm) long. An average storebought rotisserie chicken (3 lb/1.5 kg) will yield about 5 cups (1.25 L) of diced or shredded meat.

APPETIZERS

Bruschetta with Chicken, Cherry Tomatoes, and Goat Cheese

Start a summer meal with this Italian-style toasted bread, which is always a crowd favorite. For added visual appeal, use a mix of different-colored cherry tomatoes in the topping. In summer I buy them at my local farmers' market, because I know they'll be freshly picked, perfectly ripe, and sweet. Make sure you use a narrow baguette no more than 3 inches (7.5 cm) wide, so you get bite-size pieces (see Note).

Prep time: 30 minutes • Cooking time: 8 to 10 minutes • Makes: 16 bruschetta

1 baguette, cut at a slight angle in sixteen ½-inch (1.25 cm) slices

1 large garlic clove, halved

2 to 3 Tbsp (30 to 45 mL) olive oil, divided

1 cup (250 mL) diced rotisserie chicken meat

16 cherry tomatoes, quartered

8 to 10 fresh basil leaves, thinly sliced

2 tsp (10 mL) balsamic vinegar

¼ lb (125 g) soft goat cheese, pulled into small nuggets

Salt and freshly ground black pepper to taste

Freshly grated parmesan cheese to taste

1. Preheat the oven to 400°F (200°C). Arrange the bread slices in a single layer on a baking sheet and bake for 8 to 10 minutes, or until lightly toasted.

2. Allow the bread to cool for a few minutes, then rub the top of each slice with the cut side of the garlic and set on a platter. (Wrap, refrigerate, and save leftover garlic for another use.) Drizzle the toasted bread with 1 to 2 Tbsp (15 to 30 mL) of the olive oil and set aside.

3. In a bowl, combine the chicken, tomatoes, basil, 1 Tbsp (15 mL) of the olive oil, and the vinegar until well mixed.

4. Top each slice of bread with the chicken/tomato mixture and a few nuggets of the goat cheese. Season with salt and pepper, sprinkle with parmesan cheese, and serve.

Note: You can make the toasted, garlic-rubbed bread slices several hours before needed. Wrap and keep at room temperature until ready to top.

Crostini with Artichoke Pesto and Chicken

Garlicky, herbaceous, and nutty with pesto, these crostini make a simple yet delicious appetizer to dazzle guests before dinner. You can make the artichoke pesto several hours before needed and finish the crostini later in the day.

Prep time: 15 minutes • Cooking time: about 15 seconds • Makes: 16 crostini

---

1 can (14 oz/398 mL) artichoke hearts, drained well

¼ cup (60 mL) sliced almonds

½ cup (125 mL) packed fresh basil leaves

2 medium garlic cloves, sliced

⅓ cup (80 mL) freshly grated parmesan cheese

⅓ cup (80 mL) olive oil + more for the bread

Freshly ground black pepper to taste

1 baguette, cut on a slight angle in sixteen ½-inch (1.25 cm) slices

32 thin slices rotisserie chicken meat, each about 2 inches (5 cm) long and 1 inch (2.5 cm) wide

16 small fresh basil leaves

1. Place the artichokes, almonds, basil, garlic, cheese, the ⅓ cup (80 mL) of olive oil, and black pepper in the bowl of a food processor and pulse until well combined. Transfer the pesto to a bowl. (If making pesto in advance, cover and refrigerate until ready to make the crostini.)

2. Set an oven rack 6 inches (15 cm) below the broiler, then preheat the broiler to high.

3. Arrange the bread slices in a single layer on a baking sheet and brush lightly with olive oil. Broil until lightly toasted, about 15 seconds (watch the bread so it does not burn). Allow the crostini to cool to room temperature.

4. Spoon the pesto onto the crostini and arrange 2 slices of chicken on top of each one. Garnish each slice with a small basil leaf and serve.

ABOUT BRUSCHETTA AND CROSTINI

Bruschetta (broo-SKEH-tah) and crostini (kroh-STEE-nee) are both crisp, Italian-style bites made with bread, but what is the difference between the two?

The bread for bruschetta is generally cut thicker and, after being toasted, is often rubbed with garlic and drizzled with olive oil. Crostini are usually thinner, and though they may be topped with garlic, the bread is not rubbed with it.

Chicken and Brie Canapés with
Mandarin Oranges and Cranberries

Mandarin oranges and cranberries are holiday favorites, and these quick and easy canapés combine both, making them the perfect appetizer for a Christmas party. Play around with the topping; for example, try chutney instead of cranberry sauce or Camembert or Cambozola cheese in place of the brie. If you're in a hurry, these canapés can be made an hour or two before serving and refrigerated until needed.

Prep time: 10 minutes • Cooking time: none • Makes: 16 canapés

---

16 water or rice crackers

8 tsp (40 mL) mayonnaise

1 round of brie cheese (about 7 oz/200 g),
    cut in 16 small wedges

16 shreds rotisserie chicken meat, each
    about 1 inch (2.5 cm) long

16 small, fresh mandarin orange segments

8 tsp (40 mL) whole berry cranberry sauce

16 tiny sprigs of fresh parsley, for garnish

1. Arrange the crackers on a serving platter. Spread ½ tsp (2 mL) of the mayonnaise in the center of each cracker.

2. Arrange a wedge of cheese over the mayonnaise, then top with a shred of chicken, a segment of orange, and ½ tsp (2 mL) of cranberry sauce. Garnish each canapé with parsley. Cover and refrigerate the canapés until ready to serve.

Chicken and Tofu Potstickers

Potstickers are Chinese-style dumplings cooked by quickly searing and steaming them in a pan. They make a delicious snack or appetizer to enjoy before a Chinese-style meal, or any meal for that matter. Uncooked potstickers freeze well, so you can make them ahead, freeze them solid on baking sheets, transfer them to a freezer bag, and store them frozen for up to 3 months. Cook the frozen potstickers over medium heat for a minute or two longer than usual so they thaw properly and cook through without overly darkening.

Prep time: 35 to 40 minutes • Cooking time: about 6 minutes per batch • Makes: 48 potstickers

1 block (12 oz/350 g) firm tofu, drained well

½ cup (125 mL) finely diced rotisserie chicken meat

¼ cup (60 mL) grated carrots

¼ cup (60 mL) chopped fresh cilantro

1 large garlic clove, minced

1 Tbsp (15 mL) soy sauce

2 tsp (10 mL) finely chopped fresh ginger

1 tsp (5 mL) Asian-style hot chili sauce (page 88)

2 tsp (10 mL) cornstarch

48 Chinese-style round dumpling wrappers (see Note)

4 to 5 Tbsp (60 to 75 mL) vegetable oil for cooking

Rice vinegar, soy sauce, and Asian-style hot chili sauce, for dipping, to taste

1. Preheat the oven to 200°F (95°C). Have on hand a small bowl of cold water. Line a large baking sheet with parchment paper or plastic wrap.

2. Set a fine-mesh sieve over a bowl. Crumble the tofu into very small pieces over the sieve. Allow the tofu to rest for 10 minutes so any excess water can drip out. Discard the liquid.

3. Combine the tofu, chicken, carrots, cilantro, garlic, soy sauce, ginger, chili sauce, and cornstarch in a medium bowl and toss until well mixed.

4. Arrange a dumpling wrapper on a clean work surface. Dip your index finger in the cold water and lightly moisten the edges of the wrapper. Place a heaping teaspoonful (5 mL plus) of the chicken/tofu mixture in the center of the wrapper. Fold one side of the wrapper over the filling, pushing out any air and tightly pressing the edges of the wrapper together to form sealed half-moons. (If you prefer, crimp the edges of the dumpling for a more decorative look.) Set the dumpling on the prepared baking sheet.

5. Repeat with the remaining wrappers and filling. Ensure the potstickers do not touch one another on the baking sheet or they will stick together.

6. Heat 1 Tbsp (15 mL) of the vegetable oil in a large, heavy, nonstick or cast-iron skillet over medium-high heat. Add 12 to 18 potstickers, in batches, if necessary, and cook until golden on the bottom. Do not turn the dumplings. Keeping your face away from the pan to avoid splatters, carefully pour in 3 Tbsp (45 mL) of water. Cover and cook for 4 minutes, gently swirling the pan from time to time.

7. Remove the lid and continue cooking until the liquid has almost completely evaporated, and the potstickers are softened and heated through, about 2 minutes. Transfer the cooked potstickers to the baking sheet and keep warm in the oven.

8. Repeat with the remaining potstickers, adding 1 Tbsp (15 mL) of vegetable oil to the pan with each new batch.

9. Serve with rice vinegar, soy sauce, and hot chili sauce so guests can flavor their potstickers as desired.

Note: Round Chinese-style dumpling wrappers are about 4 inches (10 cm) wide and are sold in the produce section of some supermarkets. You'll also find them at Chinese or Asian food stores.

HOW TO BUY AND STORE FRESH GINGER

When buying pieces of fresh ginger, opt for firm, fairly smooth-skinned pieces of this root. Avoid shriveled and dry ones with spongy spots, sure signs that the root is old or has been improperly stored.

To keep ginger fresh, place the unpeeled root in a resealable plastic bag and refrigerate in your crisper drawer for up to 3 weeks. If you bought a supply of ginger that will last longer than that, it can also be frozen in resealable plastic bags for up to 2 months. Slice, chop, or grate frozen ginger before it is soft and thawed.

You can also preserve ginger in alcohol. Peel and slice the ginger; place it in a sterilized jar; cover it with an alcohol, such as sake, vodka, or dry sherry; seal tightly; and refrigerate for 1 month or more. Note that both freezing ginger and storing it in alcohol will alter its flavor.

Chicken Avocado Sushi Rolls

Sushi makes a great appetizer for a potluck or a Japanese-style meal, and this recipe is perfect for folks who don't eat raw fish. Double or triple the recipe if you're feeding a large group, and add some Asian-style hot chili sauce to the mayonnaise if you prefer a spicier roll. Sushi is best served fresh.

Prep time: 30 to 40 minutes • Cooking time: 20 minutes • Makes: 24 pieces

Sushi rice

3 Tbsp (45 mL) rice vinegar

1½ Tbsp (22.5 mL) granulated sugar

1½ tsp (7 mL) salt

1¾ cups (425 mL) sushi rice (see Note)

2½ cups (625 mL) cold water

Chicken and avocado filling

2 tsp (10 mL) lime juice

1 small ripe avocado

3 nori sheets (see Note)

3 Tbsp (45 mL) mayonnaise

16 to 20 pieces shredded rotisserie
chicken meat

½ cup (125 mL) teriyaki or soy sauce

Wasabi paste and pickled ginger to
taste (optional)

Note: Sushi rice, nori (thin sheets of seaweed), and teriyaki sauce are available at most supermarkets and Asian food stores. A sushi mat is made from thin lengths of bamboo held together with string. They are widely available in Asian markets and well-stocked kitchenware stores.

Sushi rice

1. Combine the vinegar, sugar, and salt in a small pot over high heat. Bring to a boil for 15 seconds, stir to dissolve the sugar, then remove from the heat and set aside until needed.

2. Place the rice in a medium bowl, cover with cold water, and rub the grains together to remove any excess starch. Drain the rice and repeat twice more.

3. Place the drained rice in a medium pot, add the 2½ cups (625 mL) of cold water, and bring to a boil over high heat. Reduce the heat to its lowest setting, cover, and cook until the rice is tender, 15 to 18 minutes.

4. Using a wooden spoon, spread the rice into a thin layer in a large, shallow-sided pan. Pour in the vinegar mixture, lifting the rice gently and continuously until it is well mixed and cooled to room temperature.

cont'd overleaf

Chicken and avocado filling

1. Have on hand a small bowl of water and a sushi mat covered with plastic wrap (see Note).

2. Spread the lime juice on a wide plate. Quarter the avocado lengthwise, pull it apart, and discard the pit. Remove and discard the peel from the avocado. Cut each quarter piece of avocado, lengthwise, into 3 slices. Set the avocado on the plate and coat with the lime juice.

3. Place a sheet of nori on the sushi mat and set it parallel to the edge of the counter. Dip your fingers in the water, then mound ⅓ of the rice on top. Using your fingers, gently spread the rice over the nori, leaving a 1-inch (2.5 cm) strip at the top.

4. Arrange 1 Tbsp (15 mL) of the mayonnaise in a thin horizontal line about ⅓ of the way from the bottom edge of the nori. Top with 4 wedges of avocado and 4 or 5 pieces of shredded chicken.

5. Starting at the edge closest to the edge of the counter, tightly roll the nori over the filling, being sure to leave the plastic wrap behind but squeezing the mat as you go to compact the rice and the filling. Continue rolling until you reach the top edge. Dip your finger in the water, run it along the top edge of the nori, and press it into the roll to seal the edge. Using a very sharp knife, cut the roll into 8 pieces and set on a serving platter.

6. Repeat twice more with the remaining nori, rice, mayonnaise, avocado, and chicken. Serve the sushi with a bowl of teriyaki or soy sauce on the side for dipping. And, if desired, add dabs of wasabi paste and pickled ginger to further flavor the sushi.

Mini Chicken and Vegetable Quiches

These two- to three-bite quiches are nice to bring to a potluck brunch or other party, as you can nibble on them and still have room to enjoy the other dishes being served.

Prep time: 20 minutes • Cooking time: about 35 minutes • Makes: 12 quiches

1 Tbsp (15 mL) olive oil

⅓ cup (80 mL) finely diced red bell peppers

⅓ cup (80 mL) diced zucchini

⅓ cup (80 mL) grated carrots

2 green onions, very thinly sliced

½ cup (125 mL) finely diced rotisserie chicken meat

¼ tsp (1 mL) dried tarragon

12 frozen tart shells, each 3 inches (7.5 cm), thawed

2 large eggs, beaten

⅓ cup (80 mL) milk or whipping cream

Salt and white pepper to taste

Pinch of ground nutmeg

½ cup (125 mL) grated Swiss or aged white cheddar cheese

1. Heat the olive oil in a skillet over medium heat. Add the bell peppers, zucchini, and carrots and cook until softened, about 5 minutes. Remove from the heat, stir in the green onions, chicken, and tarragon, and then set aside.

2. Preheat the oven to 375°F (190°C). Line a baking sheet with parchment paper. Prick each tart shell a few times with a fork and set on the baking sheet. Bake for 10 minutes and then remove from the oven. Leave the oven on.

3. While the tart shells bake, in a small bowl or a glass measuring cup, combine the eggs, milk (or cream), salt, pepper, and nutmeg.

4. Divide the vegetable/chicken mixture among the tart shells. Carefully pour in the egg mixture, then top each quiche with some of the cheese. Bake for 15 to 20 minutes, or until the eggs are set and the pastry is golden. Serve hot or at room temperature.

ABOUT BELL PEPPERS

Bell peppers, also called sweet peppers, are named for their bell-like shape.

Green bell peppers are immature peppers that are thinly fleshed and have a slightly bitter taste.

Red, yellow, and orange bell peppers are simply green bell peppers that have been allowed to fully ripen and turn their true color. Because they've ripened longer, they have a thicker, sweeter-tasting flesh.

Use green bell peppers for flavoring tomato-based sauces and stews. Sweeter and thicker red, orange, and yellow bell peppers can be eaten raw, are fine for roasting and peeling, and add visual appeal to any dish.

Chili Chicken Mini Tostadas

These spicy little bites are perfect while watching the game or enjoying a cold beer. To make a lower-fat version, use no-fat or low-fat mayonnaise and/or sour cream.

Prep time: 30 minutes • Cooking time: about 10 minutes • Makes: 24 mini tostadas

1½ cups (375 mL) diced rotisserie chicken meat

⅓ cup (80 mL) mayonnaise

¼ cup (60 mL) finely chopped green bell peppers

1 tsp (5 mL) hot pepper sauce, such as Tabasco

2 tsp (10 mL) lime juice, or to taste

½ tsp (2 mL) ground cumin

2 flour tortillas, each 10 inches (25 cm) in diameter

Vegetable oil for frying

3 Tbsp (45 mL) sour cream

24 small sprigs of fresh cilantro, for garnish

1. Combine the chicken, mayonnaise, bell peppers, hot pepper sauce, lime juice, and cumin in a bowl. Cover and refrigerate until needed. (The chicken mixture can be made several hours in advance.)

2. To make the tostadas, arrange the tortillas on a cutting board. Use a 2-inch (5 cm) round cookie cutter to cut 12 rounds from each tortilla.

3. Line a large plate with paper towels. Pour ⅛ inch (about 3 mm) of vegetable oil into a large deep skillet and heat over medium to medium-high heat. Cook the tortillas, in batches, until golden and crispy, about 30 seconds per side. Using a slotted spoon, transfer each cooked tortilla to the paper towels to drain. Arrange the cooked tortillas on a serving platter, cover with plastic wrap, and set aside at room temperature until ready to top.

4. When ready to top and serve, use a small spoon to set ½ tsp (2 mL) of sour cream in the center of each tostada. Divide the chicken mixture evenly among the tostadas, garnish with a sprig of cilantro, and serve.

Chicken Quesadillas with Quick Guacamole

These Tex-Mex–style quesadillas filled with chicken, spices, cheese, and peppers are delicious served with the ultra-easy-to-make guacamole for dipping. You can make the guacamole ahead of time and refrigerate it until needed, then mix up some margaritas, take these snacks out to the patio, and enjoy.

Prep time: 20 minutes • Cooking time: 6 minutes per batch • Makes: 4 to 6 servings

Guacamole

1 medium ripe avocado

1 Tbsp (15 mL) lime juice

¼ cup (60 mL) sour cream

½ cup (125 mL) storebought tomato salsa

Chicken quesadillas

1 ½ cups (375 mL) diced rotisserie
   chicken meat

½ tsp (2 mL) chili powder

½ tsp (2 mL) ground cumin

Salt and freshly ground black pepper
   to taste

1 medium red bell pepper, finely chopped

1 medium fresh jalapeño pepper,
   seeds removed, flesh finely chopped
   (optional)

2 cups (500 mL) grated Monterey Jack
   cheese

¼ cup (60 mL) chopped fresh cilantro or
   thinly sliced green onions

4 flour tortillas, each 10 inches (25 cm)
   in diameter

Guacamole

1. Quarter the avocado lengthwise, pull it apart, and discard the pit. Remove and discard the peel. Place the avocado flesh in a bowl with the lime juice. Using a fork, mash the avocado into small chunks.

2. Stir in the sour cream and salsa. Cover with plastic wrap and refrigerate.

Chicken quesadillas

1. In a medium bowl, combine the chicken, chili powder, cumin, and salt and pepper until well mixed. Stir in the bell peppers, jalapeño peppers, cheese, and cilantro (or green onions) and toss to combine.

2. Arrange the tortillas on a clean work surface, then spread ¼ of the chicken mixture across the bottom half of each one. Fold the top half of the tortilla over the bottom half and gently press down to spread out the filling.

3. Preheat the oven to 200°F (95°C). Set a large, wide nonstick skillet over medium to medium-high heat. (Or preheat a nonstick electric griddle to the same temperature.)

4. Cook 2 of the stuffed tortillas until the cheese is melted and the tortillas are golden, about 3 minutes per side. Transfer to a baking sheet and keep warm in the oven while you cook the second batch.

5. Cut the cooked quesadillas into 4 to 6 wedges and arrange on a platter. Serve with the guacamole.

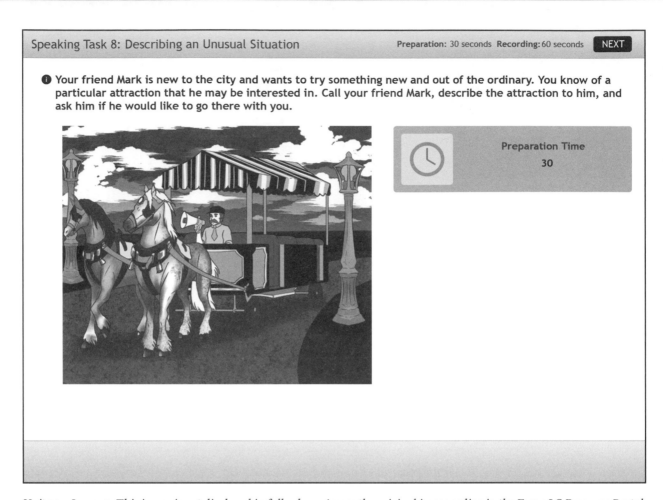

Speaking Task 8: Describing an Unusual Situation   Preparation: 30 seconds Recording: 60 seconds   NEXT

ⓘ Your friend Mark is new to the city and wants to try something new and out of the ordinary. You know of a particular attraction that he may be interested in. Call your friend Mark, describe the attraction to him, and ask him if he would like to go there with you.

Preparation Time
30

Unit 14 – Image 1: This image is not displayed in full colour. Access the original image online in the Focus LS Resource Portal.

Using Descriptive Vocabulary

In Speaking Task 8, it is important to be descriptive and precise in order to effectively convey important details in the image. If you have a basic vocabulary, you can combine simple words and phrases to express higher-level meaning. For example, if you don't know the word "yacht," this could be described in simple language as a "large sailing boat."

Those with a broader range of vocabulary can use more specific words to express precise meaning. For the example from the previous paragraph, you could add more details about the yacht, and describe it as "a luxury sailing yacht with a prominent open upper deck featuring dining tables and lounge chairs."

Activity 1

Use the image above to practice different ways of describing important things in the image. For each item, use descriptive phrases to give both a simple and a detailed description of that item. The first question has been completed for you.

Remember to access the full-colour version of this image in the Focus LS Portal.

132

Chicken and Mango Chutney Phyllo Bundles

These bite-size bundles of crispy phyllo are filled with an Indian-style curried chicken mixture. Choose a smooth chutney, not an overly chunky one that could poke holes in the phyllo. The bundles can be made oven-ready a few hours in advance and baked when your guests arrive. Securely wrap the tray of bundles with plastic wrap while you wait to ensure that the phyllo pastry does not dry out.

Prep time: 25 minutes • Cooking time: 15 minutes • Makes: 24 bundles

3 Tbsp (45 mL) sweet mango chutney

¼ lb (125 g) spreadable cream cheese

½ tsp (2 mL) mild, medium, or hot curry powder

½ cup (125 mL) very finely diced rotisserie chicken meat

2 Tbsp (30 mL) chopped fresh mint or cilantro or 1 green onion, very thinly sliced

6 sheets phyllo pastry

¼ cup (60 mL) butter, melted

Plain thick yogurt, for dipping

PHYLLO PASTRY

To use phyllo in this recipe, thaw the package overnight in the refrigerator. (If you forget, you can also thaw it at cool room temperature. It should take about 3 to 4 hours to thaw.) Phyllo is delicate and dries out quickly, so have all of your ingredients ready to go before unpacking the sheets and when you do, work quickly. Butter the sheets with a soft-bristled pastry brush, not a firm one which can cause tears.

1. Set an oven rack in the middle of the oven, then preheat the oven to 375°F (190°C). Line a baking sheet with parchment paper and set aside.

2. Combine the chutney, cream cheese, and curry powder in a bowl, then mix in the chicken and mint (or cilantro or green onions) and stir until well mixed. Set aside.

3. Arrange a sheet of phyllo on a clean work surface and brush it lightly with melted butter. Top with another sheet and brush it lightly with butter. Repeat with a third sheet of phyllo.

4. Cut the layered sheets into 12 squares. Set 2 tsp (10 mL) of the chicken filling into the center of each square. Gather the corners of each square, bring them together over the filling, and firmly squeeze them together to seal the bundle. Place the bundles on the prepared baking sheet.

5. Layer and butter 3 more sheets of phyllo, fill them with the remaining filling, and form them into 12 more bundles. Set them on the baking sheet. (The bundles can be made to this point, covered, and refrigerated for up to 8 hours until ready to bake.) Bake for 15 minutes, or until light golden. Serve with a bowl of plain yogurt for dipping.

Chicken and Fresh Corn Fritters with Chili Lime Dip

These addictive fritters are perfect as a pre-dinner snack with a glass of cold lemonade or iced tea. Make these bites in summer when corn is at its peak (see Note).

Prep time: 30 minutes • Cooking time: 3 to 4 minutes per batch • Makes: about 24 fritters

Chili lime dip

¾ cup (175 mL) mayonnaise

3 Tbsp (45 mL) chopped fresh cilantro

1 tsp (5 mL) chili powder

⅛ tsp (0.5 mL) cayenne pepper

1 Tbsp (15 mL) lime juice

2 tsp (10 mL) honey

Corn fritters

1 large egg

½ cup (125 mL) buttermilk

¾ cup (175 mL) all-purpose flour

2 tsp (10 mL) baking powder

½ tsp (2 mL) salt

⅛ tsp (0.5 mL) cayenne pepper

⅛ tsp (0.5 mL) paprika

1 cup (250 mL) finely diced rotisserie chicken meat

¾ cup (175 mL) raw, fresh corn kernels (about 1 ear)

½ cup (125 mL) thinly sliced green onions

Vegetable oil for frying

Chili lime dip

1. In a small bowl, combine all the ingredients until well mixed. Cover and refrigerate until needed. Dip can be made several hours in advance of serving.

Corn fritters

1. Preheat a deep fryer to 350°F (180°C). Preheat the oven to 200°F (95°C). Set a baking rack over a baking sheet.

2. Beat the egg in a medium bowl until well blended. Whisk in the buttermilk and set aside.

3. In a second bowl, combine the flour, baking powder, salt, cayenne, and paprika until well mixed. Stir in the chicken, corn, and green onions and toss until well coated with the flour mixture.

4. Add the flour mixture into the egg/buttermilk mixture, and mix well to create a very thick batter.

5. Working in batches, carefully drop heaping tablespoonfuls (15 mL plus) of the batter into the oil. Deep-fry until golden, 3 to 4 minutes. Using a slotted spoon, transfer the cooked fritters to the baking rack and keep warm in the oven until all the fritters are cooked.

6. Arrange the fritters on a platter and serve with a bowl of the dip alongside.

Note: Using fresh corn, cut from the cob with a sharp paring knife, will yield the best results. Although frozen kernels don't have the same fresh taste, you could use them in this recipe. Thaw them, and thoroughly pat them dry before using.

SOUPS

Chicken Stock

After enjoying the meat on a rotisserie chicken, save and freeze the carcass. Once you have three of them, you'll be able to make this homemade chicken stock, which is a great base for soups or other dishes, such as stews.

Prep time: 20 minutes, plus chilling time • Cooking time: about 2 hours • Makes: 7 to 8 cups (1.75 to 2 L)

3 rotisserie chicken carcasses, each
    broken or cut in 3 or 4 pieces
2 celery stalks, sliced
1 medium onion, peeled, halved, and sliced
1 medium carrot, peeled and sliced
2 garlic cloves, sliced
2 bay leaves
A few whole black peppercorns
A few sprigs of fresh parsley and thyme

1. Place all the ingredients in a stockpot and pour in 12 cups (3 L) of cold water. Bring to a gentle simmer (small bubbles should just break on the surface) over medium to medium-high heat. Reduce the heat, as needed, to maintain a gentle simmer. Cook, uncovered, for 2 hours. Use a spoon to skim any foam that rises to the surface.

2. Ladle a little of the stock into a small bowl, season with salt and pepper, and taste it. If it has a pleasing flavor, the stock is ready; if not, simmer the stock a few minutes longer, until it has a rich flavor.

3. To quickly and safely cool the stock, fill your sink with a mix of ice and cold water. Place a fine-mesh sieve over a clean stockpot, then strain the stock through the sieve. Discard the solids. Set the pot of strained stock in the sink, adding more ice and cold water if necessary to match the level of the stock in the pot. Allow the stock to cool to room temperature, stirring it gently every so often.

4. Cover the stock and refrigerate overnight. The next morning, use a spoon to remove any fat from the surface before using. If you don't need the stock right away, it keeps very well frozen in airtight containers. Pour your stock into the container, label and date it, and freeze for up to 3 months.

Creamy Chicken and Leek Soup

A leek is kind of like three vegetables in one. It looks like a giant scallion, is related to both garlic and onions, and has a mild and appealing flavor with hints of all three. As you'll see when tasting this soup, it goes very well with chicken.

Prep time: 10 minutes • Cooking time: about 25 minutes • Makes: 4 servings

3 Tbsp (45 mL) olive oil

1 medium leek, white and light green
    parts only, halved lengthwise, washed,
    and thinly sliced

2 medium garlic cloves, minced

¼ cup (60 mL) all-purpose flour

1 tsp (5 mL) dried tarragon

3½ cups (875 mL) chicken stock (page 59)

1½ cups (375 mL) diced rotisserie
    chicken meat

1 cup (250 mL) whole milk or light cream

Salt and white pepper to taste

⅓ cup (80 mL) crumbled blue cheese,
    for garnish (optional)

1. Heat the olive oil in a stockpot over medium heat. Add the leeks and garlic and cook until softened, about 5 minutes.

2. Stir in the flour and tarragon and cook for 2 minutes more. Using a whisk, slowly stir in the stock until well combined. Mix in the chicken. Allow the soup to come to a gentle simmer and cook for 15 minutes, until lightly thickened and rich tasting.

3. Pour in the milk (or cream) and heat through for 2 minutes. Season with salt and pepper and serve, garnished with blue cheese (if using).

HOW TO CLEAN A LEEK

Most supermarkets sell medium to large leeks, which are large enough to have developed layers where dirt can become trapped. Because of that, it's important that you carefully wash leeks before using them.

Start by trimming off the hairy-looking root end and the more fibrous, darkest green top portion that grows above ground and is tough in texture. Now cut the trimmed leek in half lengthwise, exposing the places where dirt can get trapped. Wash thoroughly under cold running water to remove any dirt, pat the leek dry, and it's ready to cut and use as needed. The upper portion that you trimmed away, after washing, could be sliced and used in place of onions to flavor chicken stock (page 59).

Country-style Chicken and Cabbage Soup

This hearty, chunky soup makes a deliciously satisfying meal for even the hungriest, hardest-working farmhand, particularly when served with Cheddar–Green Onion Wedge Biscuits (page 186). For an Italian version of this soup, omit the thyme and swirl in 2 to 3 Tbsp (30 to 45 mL) of pesto (page 169) just before serving.

Prep time: 25 minutes • Cooking time: about 25 minutes • Makes: 4 to 6 servings

2 Tbsp (30 mL) vegetable oil

1 large onion, diced

2 medium carrots, peeled, halved
   lengthwise, and sliced

2 medium garlic cloves, chopped

4 cups (1 L) chopped green cabbage

5 cups (1.25 L) chicken stock (page 59)

2 medium red-skinned potatoes, cubed

1 cup (250 mL) diced rotisserie
   chicken meat

½ tsp (2 mL) dried thyme

2 bay leaves

Salt and freshly ground black pepper
   to taste

1. Heat the vegetable oil in a large stockpot over medium to medium-high heat. Add the onions, carrots, and garlic and cook for 5 minutes, until softened.

2. Stir in the remaining ingredients and allow to come to a boil. Reduce the heat to low and simmer the soup gently for 15 to 20 minutes, or until the vegetables are tender. Season to taste and serve.

Eight-Vegetable Soup with Chicken

This no-fuss, throw-all-ingredients-in-the-pot, large-batch soup recipe freezes well. That makes it possible to enjoy some now and store the rest for another time when you feel like having a bowl of this nutritious soup. I like garlic and have added three large cloves to this recipe. However, feel free to adjust the amount according to your preference.

Prep time: 20 minutes • Cooking time: 25 to 30 minutes • Makes: 10 servings

2 medium onions, diced

1 cup (250 mL) fresh or frozen corn kernels

2 medium carrots, halved lengthwise and cut in ½-inch (1.25 cm) slices

2 celery stalks, diced

1 medium green bell pepper, diced

3 large garlic cloves, minced

2 medium white-skinned potatoes, cubed

4 medium ripe tomatoes, halved, seeds removed, and diced

1½ cups (375 mL) diced rotisserie chicken meat

8 cups (2 L) chicken stock (page 59)

2 bay leaves

1 tsp (5 mL) dried basil

A few pinches of dried, crushed chili flakes (optional)

Salt and freshly ground black pepper to taste

Freshly grated parmesan cheese, for garnish, to taste (optional)

1. Place all the ingredients except the parmesan cheese in a large stockpot and bring to a boil over medium-high heat.

2. Reduce the heat to low and simmer gently for 20 minutes, or until the vegetables are tender. Season with salt and pepper. If desired, serve bowls of the soup sprinkled with parmesan cheese to taste.

Chicken Noodle Soup

Serve this classic and comforting soup to soothe a cold, or just to make yourself (and others!) feel better about life on a dreary day.

Prep time: 15 minutes • Cooking time: about 25 minutes • Makes: 4 servings

1 Tbsp (15 mL) vegetable oil

½ medium onion, diced

1 medium celery stalk, quartered
   lengthwise and thinly sliced

1 small carrot, quartered lengthwise and
   thinly sliced

4 cups (1 L) chicken stock (page 59)

1 cup (250 mL) diced rotisserie
   chicken meat

1 to 1½ cups (250 to 375 mL) broad
   egg noodles

Salt and freshly ground black pepper
   to taste

1 Tbsp (15 mL) chopped fresh parsley,
   chives, or tarragon

1. Heat the vegetable oil in a stockpot over medium heat. Add the onions, celery, and carrots and cook for 5 minutes, until softened.
2. Stir in the stock and chicken, bring to a simmer, and simmer for 10 minutes.
3. Add the noodles, return the soup to a simmer, and cook until the noodles are tender, 6 to 8 minutes. Season with salt and pepper, stir in the parsley (or chives or tarragon), and serve.

Brothy Tortellini with Chicken and Kale

This hearty meal-in-a-bowl uses the packaged, ready-to-cook fresh tortellini sold at most supermarkets.

Prep time: 10 minutes • Cooking time: about 10 minutes • Makes: 4 servings

---

1 pkg (½ lb/250 g) cheese tortellini

4 cups (1 L) chicken stock (page 59)

2 cups (500 mL) cubed rotisserie
 chicken meat

3 to 4 leaves fresh kale, washed well,
 tough lower rib trimmed and
 discarded, leaves coarsely chopped

2 Tbsp (30 mL) storebought or homemade
 pesto (page 169)

Salt and freshly ground black pepper
 to taste

Dried chili flakes, for garnish, to taste
 (optional)

Freshly grated parmesan cheese, for
 garnish, to taste (optional)

1. Set a large pot of water over medium-high heat and bring to a boil. In a second pot, bring the stock to a simmer over medium to medium-high heat.

2. Add the tortellini to the boiling water and cook according to the package directions until tender.

3. While the tortellini cooks, add the chicken and kale to the stock and simmer for 5 minutes, or until the kale is tender. Stir in the pesto and salt and pepper to taste. Reduce the heat to medium-low and reserve until the tortellini is cooked.

4. Drain the tortellini well and divide among 4 wide, shallow bowls. Ladle the chicken/kale mixture over the tortellini and serve. Sprinkle with crushed chili flakes and grated parmesan cheese, if desired.

ABOUT KALE

Kale, like broccoli and cabbage, is part of the Brassica genus in the mustard family. It comes in many different varieties, including green, purple, and Russian, and is a source of vitamins such as A and C and minerals such as calcium, fiber, folic acid, and iron.

In supermarkets, kale is most often sold with its frilly leaves tied in a bouquet-like bunch. Choose fresh, crisp-looking bunches with moist stems and, preferably, smaller, therefore more tender, leaves. Avoid bunches with overly tough, limp, or yellowing leaves.

Kale is fairly perishable but, if in good condition, will keep in a plastic bag in your refrigerator crisper for a few days. Wash well just before using to dislodge any dirt trapped in its leaves.

Asian-style Chicken Noodle Bowl

If you have a cold, this Asian-style chicken soup's hot-and-sour flavors should help clear it up, at least for a little while.

Prep time: 20 minutes • Cooking time: about 10 minutes • Makes: 4 servings

5 cups (1.25 L) chicken stock (page 59)

1 large garlic clove, minced

1 Tbsp (15 mL) chopped fresh ginger

3 Tbsp (45 mL) rice vinegar

1½ tsp (7 mL) granulated sugar

2 Tbsp (30 mL) soy sauce

1 tsp (5 mL) sesame oil

2 tsp (10 mL) Asian-style hot chili sauce, or to taste (page 88)

1 cup (250 mL) diced rotisserie chicken meat

1 small red bell pepper, diced

2 to 3 baby bok choy, trimmed, separated into leaves, washed, and coarsely chopped

10½ oz (300 g) fresh Asian-style thin egg noodles (see Note)

2 green onions, thinly sliced, for garnish

2 Tbsp (30 mL) chopped fresh cilantro, for garnish

1. Set a large pot of water over medium-high heat and bring to a boil.

2. While the water comes to temperature, place the chicken stock, garlic, ginger, vinegar, sugar, soy sauce, sesame oil, chili sauce, chicken, and bell peppers in a second pot and bring to a gentle simmer over medium to medium-high heat. Simmer for 5 minutes. Add the bok choy and cook for 2 minutes more.

3. Add the noodles to the boiling water and cook until just tender, about 1 minute. Drain well and divide among 4 large soup bowls. Ladle the chicken mixture and broth over the noodles. Top with green onions and cilantro and serve.

Note: Fresh Asian-style egg noodles are sold at Asian food stores and at some supermarkets.

Lentil and Chicken Soup with Herbes de Provence

This hearty soup is enhanced with herbes de Provence (page 190), an aromatic French-style blend. Make a filling two-course meal by serving this soup followed by Leaf Lettuce Salad with Ranch Dressing, Bacon Bits, and Tomatoes (page 150) or Spinach and Vegetable Salad with Lemon-Tarragon Yogurt Dressing (page 149).

Prep time: 20 minutes • Cooking time: 20 minutes • Makes: 4 to 6 servings

2 Tbsp (30 mL) olive oil

½ medium onion, finely diced

2 celery stalks, quartered lengthwise
and thinly sliced

1 medium carrot, quartered lengthwise
and thinly sliced

1 medium garlic clove, minced

1 tsp (5 mL) herbes de Provence

4 cups (1 L) chicken stock (page 59)

1 cup (250 mL) diced rotisserie
chicken meat

1 can (19 oz/540 ml) lentils, drained
well, rinsed, and drained well again

1 can (14 oz/398 mL) diced tomatoes

Salt and freshly ground black pepper
to taste

2 Tbsp (30 mL) chopped fresh parsley,
for garnish

1. Heat the olive oil in a stockpot over medium heat. Add the onions, celery, and carrots and cook for 5 minutes, until softened. Stir in the garlic and herbes de Provence and cook for 1 minute more.

2. Add the stock, chicken, lentils, and tomatoes and bring to a gentle simmer. Simmer for 15 minutes, then season with salt and pepper and serve. Garnish individual soup bowls with a small spoonful of parsley swirled into the soup.

Chicken, Kale, and Bean Soup

This sustaining soup makes a nice winter lunch served with Soda Bread with Oats, Walnuts, and Thyme (page 189). It also freezes well: allow the soup to cool to room temperature, pour it into an airtight container, and freeze for up to 3 months. To eat, just thaw, heat, and enjoy. If you're not fond of kidney beans, substitute an equal amount of chickpeas or romano beans or any other bean you prefer.

Prep time: 20 minutes • Cooking time: about 30 minutes • Makes: 6 servings

2 Tbsp (30 mL) olive oil

1 small onion, finely chopped

1 medium carrot, finely chopped

1 medium celery stalk, finely chopped

2 medium garlic cloves, minced

2 Tbsp (30 mL) tomato paste

1 tsp (5 mL) dried oregano

5 cups (1.25 L) chicken stock (page 59)

1 ½ cups (375 mL) diced rotisserie
   chicken meat

1 can (19 oz/540 mL) white kidney beans,
   drained well, rinsed, and drained
   well again

1 can (14 oz/398 mL) diced tomatoes

4 leaves fresh kale, washed well, tough
   middle rib trimmed and
   discarded, leaves coarsely chopped
   (page 65)

Salt and freshly ground black pepper
   to taste

Freshly grated parmesan cheese, for
   garnish, to taste

Dried, crushed chili flakes, for garnish,
   to taste (optional)

1. Heat the olive oil in a stockpot over medium heat. Add the onions, carrots, celery, and garlic and cook until tender, about 5 minutes.

2. Stir in the tomato paste and oregano and cook for 1 minute more.

3. Add the stock, chicken, beans, and tomatoes, then allow the soup to come to a gentle simmer. Simmer for 20 minutes.

4. Stir in the kale and cook until tender, about 5 minutes. Season with salt and pepper, and then ladle into bowls. At the table, garnish with parmesan cheese and, if desired, chili flakes.

Tortilla Soup with Chicken, Avocado, and Cheese

Among the numerous variations of this popular Mexican-style soup, this version is one of the easiest to make. It requires a bit, but not a mountain, of chopping, but the results are flavorful and filling. Freeze this soup—without the garnishes—for a rainy day. Pour it into an airtight container and freeze for up to 3 months. Just thaw, reheat, and top before serving.

Prep time: 30 minutes • Cooking time: about 35 minutes • Makes: 6 servings

Tortilla strips

9 fresh corn tortillas, each 6 inches (15 cm)
   in diameter (see Note)
2 Tbsp (30 mL) vegetable oil
½ tsp (2 mL) ground cumin
½ tsp (2 mL) chili powder

Note: Fresh corn tortillas are available in the refrigerated section of most supermarkets. Look for fresh, dark green, mildly spicy poblano peppers in the produce section. If you can't find them, use a medium green bell pepper instead.

Tortilla soup

2 Tbsp (30 mL) olive oil
1 medium onion, diced
1 medium fresh poblano pepper, diced (see Note)
1 small to medium jalapeño pepper, halved, seeds
   removed, flesh chopped
1 garlic clove, minced
4 cups (1 L) chicken stock (page 59)
1 can (28 oz/796 mL) diced tomatoes
1 Tbsp (15 mL) fresh lime juice
Pinch of granulated sugar
1 ½ to 2 cups (375 to 500 mL) thinly shredded
   rotisserie chicken meat
Salt to taste
1 large ripe avocado, quartered lengthwise, peeled,
   pitted, and cut in small cubes
⅓ cup (80 mL) chopped fresh cilantro
1½ cups (375 mL) grated Monterey Jack cheese,
   or to taste
1 or 2 limes, cut in wedges

Tortilla strips

1. Preheat the oven to 375°F (190°C). Line a large baking sheet with parchment paper and a small plate with paper towels.

2. Cut each tortilla in half. Cut each half tortilla, widthwise, into strips ¼ inch (6 mm) wide and set in a bowl. Add the vegetable oil, cumin, and chili powder and toss to combine.

3. Arrange the tortilla strips in a single layer on the prepared baking sheet. Bake for 10 minutes, then give the tortilla strips a stir. Bake for 5 minutes more, or until golden and crispy. Transfer the tortilla strips to the paper towels to drain. Set aside until needed.

Tortilla soup

1. Heat the olive oil in a stockpot over medium heat. Add the onions, peppers, and garlic and cook until tender, about 5 minutes.

2. Stir in the stock, tomatoes, lime juice, and sugar and allow to come to a gentle simmer. Cook for 10 minutes.

3. Transfer the soup to a food processor or a blender and purée until smooth (or purée in the pot using an immersion blender). Add a bit more stock if the soup is too thick. (The soup can be made to this point, allowed to cool to room temperature, and refrigerated in an airtight container for up to 1 day.)

4. When ready to serve, heat the soup over medium heat, stir in the chicken, and bring to a simmer. Season with salt to taste.

5. Place the tortilla strips, avocado, cilantro, cheese, and lime wedges into separate bowls and set on the dinner table. Ladle the soup into individual bowls and allow guests to garnish their soup with the toppings, as desired.

HOW TO MEASURE GRATED AND CRUMBLED CHEESES

When purchasing firmer cheeses, such as cheddar or Swiss, it's handy to know that 3½ to 4 oz (100 to 125 g) yields about 1 cup (250 mL) grated (when using the largest holes on your grater). Placing semi-firm cheeses, such as Monterey Jack and mozzarella, in the freezer for 10 minutes or so to firm up makes grating them much easier. When purchasing softer cheeses, such as blue or feta (goat cheese), count on 6 oz (175 g) to yield about 1 cup (250 mL) crumbled.

Quinoa Soup with Chicken, Squash, and Pesto

Easy to make and full of nutritious quinoa and squash, this soup uses chunks of cleaned banana squash, sold in the produce department of most supermarkets. If you can't find it, use any other peeled and cubed squash that appeals, such as butternut. Or peel and cube a large yam (about 1 lb/500 g) and add it to the soup instead.

Prep time: 15 minutes • Cooking time: about 25 minutes • Makes: 6 servings

---

2 Tbsp (30 mL) olive oil

½ small onion, finely chopped

1 medium celery stalk, finely chopped

4 cups (1 L) chicken stock (page 59) or
   vegetable stock

1 cup (250 mL) diced rotisserie
   chicken meat

1 lb (500 g) cleaned banana squash, peeled
   and cut in ½-inch (1.25 cm) cubes

⅓ cup (80 mL) quinoa

1 can (14 oz/398 mL) diced tomatoes

2 Tbsp (30 mL) storebought or homemade
   pesto (page 169)

Salt and freshly ground black pepper
   to taste

1. Heat the olive oil in a stockpot over medium heat. Add the onions and celery and cook for 5 minutes, until softened.

2. Stir in the stock, chicken, squash, quinoa, and tomatoes and bring to a gentle simmer. Simmer for 15 to 18 minutes, or until the squash and quinoa are tender.

3. Stir in the pesto, season with salt and pepper, and serve.

ABOUT QUINOA

Quinoa, pronounced "KEEN-wah," is an ancient food that was a staple for the Inca. In the modern world it has become popular again because it is high in fiber, a complete source of protein, and a complex (good) carbohydrate. Quinoa contains all eight essential amino acids and is abundant in linolenic acid, an essential fatty acid said to benefit immune response. It also contains iron, calcium, vitamin E, riboflavin, and potassium, and is gluten free.

Quinoa looks like a grain—and is often referred to as a grain—but is actually a tiny seed harvested from a plant native to the Andes. The seeds come in a range of colors, such as black and red, but the white or golden ones are most common. No matter what the color, the seeds cook up in the same amount of time and can be used interchangeably or in combination.

Slow-cooker Mulligatawny Soup

This Anglo-Indian curry-spiced soup is richly stocked with chicken, vegetables, apples, and rice. Make a meal of this soup by serving it with storebought pita bread or naan, or with Cumin Seed Chapattis (page 185). You will need a slow cooker with at least a 5-quart (5 litre) capacity to make this recipe.

Prep time: 25 minutes • Cooking time: 6 hours and 20 minutes • Makes: 8 servings

1½ cups (375 mL) diced rotisserie chicken meat

1 medium onion, diced

1 medium carrot, diced

1 medium celery stalk, diced

1 small red bell pepper, diced

2 medium garlic cloves, minced

4 tsp (20 mL) mild or medium curry powder

1 large, green apple, unpeeled but diced

2 tsp (10 mL) finely grated lime zest

2 Tbsp (30 mL) freshly squeezed lime juice

1 Tbsp (15 mL) honey

1 bay leaf

4 cups (1 L) chicken stock (page 59)

2 Tbsp (30 mL) cornstarch dissolved in ½ cup (125 mL) water

1 cup (250 mL) cooked white or brown rice

¼ cup (60 mL) chopped fresh cilantro or parsley

1 can (14 oz/398 mL) coconut milk

Salt to taste

⅓ cup (80 mL) sliced almonds, lightly roasted (optional)

1. Combine the chicken, onions, carrots, celery, bell peppers, garlic, curry powder, apples, lime zest and juice, honey, bay leaf, stock, and the cornstarch/water mixture in your slow cooker. Cover and cook on the low setting for 6 hours.

2. Stir in the rice, cilantro (or parsley), and coconut milk. Cover and cook for 20 minutes more, or until all the ingredients are hot. Season the soup with salt. If desired, top with a few toasted almonds.

Hot and Sour Soup with Chicken

Served for lunch or dinner on a cool day, this aromatic, chili-spiced, Chinese-style soup will bring comfort and awaken positive spirits, not to mention your palate.

Prep time: 25 minutes • Cooking time: 8 to 10 minutes • Makes: 4 servings

4 cups (1 L) chicken stock (page 59)

¼ cup (60 mL) rice vinegar

3 Tbsp (45 mL) light soy sauce

1 Tbsp (15 mL) Asian-style hot chili sauce, or to taste (page 88)

2 tsp (10 mL) granulated sugar

1 cup (250 mL) diced rotisserie chicken meat

4 large fresh shiitake mushrooms or 4 dried black Chinese mushrooms (soaked in warm water for 20 minutes to soften), tough stems removed and discarded, caps thinly sliced

1 small carrot, cut in thin, 1-inch (2.5 cm) strips

1-inch (2.5 cm) piece fresh ginger, peeled, sliced, and cut in thin strips

1 garlic clove, chopped

2 Tbsp (30 mL) cornstarch

3 Tbsp (45 mL) water

½ pkg (10½ oz/300 g) soft tofu, cut in small cubes

2 green onions, thinly sliced, or ¼ cup (60 mL) chopped fresh cilantro, for garnish

1. Place the stock, vinegar, soy sauce, chili sauce, and sugar in a stockpot and bring to a boil over high heat.

2. Add the chicken, mushrooms, carrots, ginger, and garlic, and reduce the heat to low. Simmer gently for 5 minutes, or until the mushrooms and carrots are just tender.

3. Combine the cornstarch and water in a bowl, then slowly stir the mixture into the pot. Add the tofu and simmer until the soup is slightly thickened, 2 to 3 minutes.

4. Ladle the soup into 4 bowls, sprinkle with green onions (or cilantro), and serve.

SALADS

Salad Greens with Chicken, Grapefruit, Cranberries, and Hemp Heart Dressing

This light and refreshing main-course salad is stunning to look at, thanks to its colorful ingredients. Better yet, its citrus dressing is enhanced with hemp hearts, which give it a slightly nutty flavor and a healthy dose of essential fatty acids, protein, and fiber. Look for hemp hearts, shelled hemp seeds about the size of sesame seeds, at health food stores and some supermarkets. If you can't find them, use lightly toasted sesame seeds instead.

Prep time: 20 minutes • Cooking time: none • Makes: 4 servings

Hemp heart dressing

¼ cup (60 mL) plain thick yogurt

2 Tbsp (30 mL) orange juice

2 Tbsp (30 mL) grapefruit juice

2 tsp (10 mL) honey

2 tsp (10 mL) Dijon mustard

Pinch of dried tarragon

1 Tbsp (15 mL) hemp hearts

Salt and freshly ground black pepper
 to taste

Salad

2 small to medium red grapefruits

8 cups (2 L) mixed baby salad greens

1½ to 2 cups (375 to 500 mL) shredded
 rotisserie chicken meat

⅓ cup (80 mL) dried cranberries

⅓ cup (80 mL) grated carrots

Hemp heart dressing

1. In a small bowl, whisk together the yogurt, orange juice, grapefruit juice, honey, mustard, tarragon, and hemp hearts until well combined. Season with salt and pepper. Cover and refrigerate dressing until needed. It can be made several hours in advance.

Salad

1. Using a sharp paring knife, cut and discard a thin slice from the blossom and bottom ends of 1 grapefruit, then set it, one of the cut sides down, on a clean work surface. Following the curved contour of the fruit, carefully cut off and discard the peel and the pith.
2. Cut the grapefruit in half vertically, then very carefully cut each half into thin slices. Repeat with the second grapefruit.
3. Arrange the slices around the perimeter of 4 plates. Mound ¼ of the salad greens in the center of each plate, then top with the chicken, cranberries, and carrots. Drizzle with dressing and serve.

Dinner Salad with Homemade Ranch Dressing

This cool "meal on a plate" is rich with sliced chicken, goat cheese, blanched beans, crisp lettuce, and a creamy and tangy homemade ranch dressing. Refrigerate and save any leftover ranch dressing for up to 1 week.

Prep time: 20 minutes • Cooking time: about 7 minutes (including the bacon) • Makes: 4 servings

Ranch dressing

¾ cup (175 mL) buttermilk

¼ cup (60 mL) sour cream

2 Tbsp (30 mL) mayonnaise

1 Tbsp (15 mL) chopped fresh parsley

1 green onion, finely chopped

¼ tsp (1 mL) dried oregano

1 small garlic clove, finely chopped

Salt and freshly ground black pepper
   to taste

3 strips bacon, cooked until crispy,
   drained well, and crumbled (optional)

Dinner salad

⅓ lb (about 165 g) green beans, trimmed

1 small head iceberg or romaine or leaf
   lettuce, chopped

Meat from ½ a rotisserie chicken, sliced

5 oz (150 g) soft goat cheese, pulled into
   small nuggets

16 cherry tomatoes, halved

1 small red onion, thinly sliced

Ranch dressing

1. Combine the dressing ingredients in a bowl until well mixed. The dressing can be made several hours ahead of time and covered and refrigerated until needed.

Dinner salad

1. Bring a medium pot of water to a boil over high heat. Add the green beans and cook for 1 to 2 minutes, until just tender and bright green. Drain well, run cold water into the pot, and allow to sit until the beans are cold. Drain again and set aside.

2. Divide the lettuce among 4 dinner plates. Artfully arrange the chicken, cheese, tomatoes, green beans, and red onions on top. Serve the ranch dressing in a small bowl alongside and allow guests to help themselves.

Rotisserie Chicken on White Bean and Arugula Salad

The chicken in this recipe can be served hot, or refrigerated and served cold on a warm day. Either way, it will taste delicious with the earthy, peppery-tasting salad.

Prep time: 20 minutes • Cooking time: none • Makes: 4 servings

2 Tbsp (30 mL) storebought or homemade pesto (page 169)

2 Tbsp (30 mL) olive oil

1 Tbsp (15 mL) red wine vinegar or balsamic vinegar

1 can (19 oz/540 mL) white kidney beans, drained and rinsed

3 cups (750 mL) loosely packed baby arugula

⅓ cup (80 mL) finely chopped yellow bell peppers

¼ cup (60 mL) finely chopped red onions

Salt and freshly ground black pepper to taste

1 rotisserie chicken, hot or cold, cut into portions (page 16)

8 lemon slices, cut in half, for garnish

1. Combine the pesto, olive oil, and vinegar in a medium bowl. Add the kidney beans, arugula, bell peppers, onions, and salt and pepper, and toss to combine.

2. Mound some of the bean salad on each of 4 dinner plates. Arrange the chicken on top, then garnish with lemon slices and serve.

ABOUT ARUGULA

Peppery-tasting arugula, also called rocket, is a member of the cabbage family. Baby arugula is harvested when the plant is not fully mature, so the leaves are small and less intense in flavor.

When purchasing arugula, look for crisp, emerald green leaves. If you've bought a bunch of arugula with the roots attached, wrap the roots in a slightly water-dampened piece of paper towel, place the arugula in a plastic bag, and refrigerate. If you've bought loose leaves, refrigerate them in the bag or box in which they were sold.

To prepare arugula, trim off the roots and stems just before needed and discard. Thoroughly wash the leaves and dry. Bring slightly wilted arugula leaves back to life by soaking them in a bowl of ice-cold water for 30 minutes before using, or freshen up the flavor of arugula by washing and drying the leaves again just before using.

Baby Kale Caesar Salad with Chicken

Nutritious baby kale, sold in plastic tubs at many supermarkets, is the leafy green that anchors this version of Caesar salad. Feel free to substitute baby spinach or a mix of spinach and kale or even traditional romaine lettuce, if you prefer. Topped with cubes or shreds of rotisserie chicken, this salad makes a fine main course for lunch or dinner.

Prep time: 15 minutes • Cooking time: none • Makes: 4 servings

⅓ cup (80 mL) mayonnaise

2 garlic cloves, minced

1 Tbsp (15 mL) lemon juice

1 Tbsp (15 mL) water

1 Tbsp (15 mL) olive oil

Splashes of Worcestershire and
  Tabasco sauce

2 anchovies, minced, or 1 tsp (5 mL)
  anchovy paste

1 tsp (5 mL) Dijon mustard

1 tsp (5 mL) red wine vinegar

Freshly ground black pepper to taste

1 tub (5 oz/150 g) fresh baby kale

1 to 1½ cups (250 to 375 mL) storebought
  or homemade croutons (see Note)

1½ cups (375 mL) diced or shredded
  rotisserie chicken meat

Freshly grated parmesan cheese to taste

8 lemon slices, halved, for garnish

1. To make the dressing, in a large bowl, combine the mayonnaise, garlic, lemon juice, water, olive oil, Worcestershire sauce, Tabasco sauce, anchovies, mustard, vinegar, and pepper.

2. Add the kale and croutons to the dressing and toss to coat. Divide the salad among 4 plates.

3. Arrange ¼ of the chicken meat on each salad. Sprinkle with parmesan cheese, garnish with lemon slices, and serve.

Note: To make your own croutons, heat 1 Tbsp (15 mL) of olive oil in a skillet over medium heat. Add 1 to 11/2 cups (250 to 375 mL) of cubed baguette. Cook, stirring from time to time, until the bread is lightly toasted, about 5 minutes.

Tomato and Marinated Olive Salad with Chicken

On a hot summer day, this flavorful Mediterranean-style main-course salad would be nice to enjoy on a patio. Use a variety of red, yellow, and orange tomatoes for added visual appeal. Pair this salad with a glass of rosé wine and some Focaccia Bread with Herbs and Onions (page 190), and life will be good.

Prep time: 25 minutes, plus marinating time • Cooking time: none • Makes: 4 servings

¼ cup (60 mL) pitted or unpitted
   black olives

¼ cup (60 mL) pitted or unpitted
   green olives

2 Tbsp (30 mL) extra-virgin olive oil

1 Tbsp (15 mL) balsamic vinegar

1 tsp (5 mL) finely grated orange zest

1 medium garlic clove, minced

2 Tbsp (30 mL) chopped fresh basil

6 cups (1.5 L) baby salad greens or arugula
   or spinach

4 medium ripe, red on-the-vine tomatoes,
   thinly sliced

Meat from ½ a rotisserie chicken, sliced

1. In a small bowl, combine the olives, olive oil, vinegar, orange zest, garlic, and basil. Allow the olives to marinate at room temperature for 1 hour.

2. Divide the salad greens (or arugula or spinach) among 4 dinner plates. Arrange ¼ of the tomato slices on top of the greens on each plate. Mound the chicken in the center of each salad.

3. Drain the olives, reserving the marinade. Set the olives on each salad, drizzle with some of the reserved marinade, and serve.

Old-fashioned Pasta Salad with Chicken, Pickles, and Mustard

This old-school, mayonnaise-based pasta salad is cold comfort food that will appeal to all ages. For a richer and creamier salad, replace ⅓ cup (80 mL) of the mayonnaise with sour cream. Either way, bring it to a potluck or a picnic and watch folks gobble it up.

Prep time: 20 minutes • Cooking time: about 10 minutes • Makes: 8 servings

2 cups (500 mL) rotini pasta

1½ cups (375 mL) shredded rotisserie chicken meat

½ cup (125 mL) diced celery

½ cup (125 mL) diced red bell peppers

3 green onions, thinly sliced

1 medium dill pickle, finely chopped

¾ to 1 cup (175 mL to 250 mL) mayonnaise

2 Tbsp (30 mL) yellow or Dijon mustard

2 Tbsp (30 mL) cider vinegar

2 tsp (10 mL) honey

Splash or 2 of hot pepper sauce, such as Tabasco

Splash or 2 of Worcestershire sauce

Salt and white pepper to taste

1. Bring a large pot of lightly salted water to a boil over medium-high heat. Add the pasta and cook until just tender, 8 to 10 minutes. Drain well, run cold water into the pot, and allow to sit until pasta is cold. Drain again.

2. Place the pasta in a large bowl, add the remaining ingredients, and toss gently to combine. Cover and refrigerate until ready to serve. This salad can be prepared several hours before serving.

Italian-style Pasta Salad with Chicken, Squash, and Radicchio

This full-flavored pasta salad serves twelve, making it a great item to serve at, or bring to, a large gathering, such as a potluck. To maintain the salad's vibrant color, dress it close to serving time.

Prep time: 30 minutes • Cooking time: about 10 minutes • Makes: 12 servings

⅓ cup (80 mL) olive oil

2 Tbsp (30 mL) apple cider vinegar

1 Tbsp (15 mL) honey

1 Tbsp (15 mL) Dijon mustard

2 Tbsp (30 mL) finely chopped fresh sage or basil or oregano (or a mix)

¾ lb (375 g) bowtie or rotini or penne pasta (about 4 cups/1 L)

¾ lb (375 g) banana squash, peeled, cut in ½-inch (1.25 cm) cubes, and par-boiled (see Note)

36 small broccoli florets, blanched (see Note)

½ medium head radicchio, cored, halved lengthwise, and very thinly sliced

1½ cups (375 mL) diced rotisserie chicken meat

1 cup (250 mL) grated asiago cheese

Salt and freshly ground black pepper to taste

1. To make the dressing, in a small bowl, whisk together the olive oil, vinegar, honey, mustard, and sage (or basil or oregano). Cover and refrigerate until needed. The dressing can be made several hours before you dress the salad.

2. To cook the pasta, bring a large pot of lightly salted water to a boil over medium-high heat. Add the pasta and cook until just tender, 8 to 10 minutes. Drain well, run cold water into the pot, drain well again, and transfer to a large bowl.

3. Add the squash, broccoli, radicchio, chicken, and cheese and toss gently to combine. (You can make the salad to this point several hours before needed; cover and refrigerate until ready to serve.)

4. Pour the dressing into the pasta mixture, season with salt and pepper, toss to combine, and serve.

Note: To parboil the squash, set it in a pot and cover with 2 inches (5 cm) of cold water. Bring to a simmer over medium heat and cook until just tender but still a little firm, about 5 minutes. Drain well, run cold water into the pot, and allow it to sit until the squash is cold. Drain again and add to the salad.

To blanch the broccoli, cook in boiling water for 2 minutes. Drain well, run cold water into the pot, and allow it to sit until the broccoli is cold. Drain again and add to the salad.

Asian-style Noodle Salad with Chicken and Peanuts

This noodle salad is always a winner when I bring it to a gathering. In fact, I sometimes make a double batch just to make sure there's enough. The rice noodles used in the salad are available in the Asian food aisle of most supermarkets.

Prep time: 25 minutes • Cooking time: 1 minute • Makes: 8 servings

1 pkg (½ lb/250 g) rice noodles or Asian-style thin egg noodles

1½ cups (375 mL) diced or thinly shredded rotisserie chicken meat

1 medium carrot, grated

½ English cucumber, grated

4 green onions, thinly sliced

1½ cups (375 mL) bean sprouts

2 medium garlic cloves, minced

1 Tbsp (15 mL) chopped fresh ginger

¼ cup (60 mL) light soy sauce

2 Tbsp (30 mL) sesame oil

2 Tbsp (30 mL) rice wine vinegar

1 Tbsp (15 mL) honey

½ tsp (2 mL) Asian-style hot chili sauce, or to taste

¼ cup (60 mL) chopped fresh cilantro

⅓ cup (80 mL) unsalted roasted peanuts or cashews, coarsely chopped

1. Bring a large pot of water to a boil over high heat. Add the rice noodles and cook for 1 minute, or until just tender. Drain well, and then gently rinse under cold water until cool. Drain well, and then transfer the noodles to a large bowl.

2. Add the remaining ingredients to the noodles, toss gently to combine, then refrigerate until ready to serve. Toss gently before serving.

ABOUT HOT SAUCES

Hot chili sauces come in many forms and flavors, but in this book, two main styles are used.

Asian-style hot chili sauce is made from small, hot red chili peppers and is sold in two forms: smooth and fairly thick, like Sriracha, or coarser and containing bits of chili pepper, like sambal oelek. In this book, recipes calling for Asian-style hot chili sauces all refer to the smooth Sriracha-type sauce.

North American–style hot chili sauce, called hot pepper sauce in this book, is made from a variety of hot peppers and is more liquid and vinegar-based. Examples include Tabasco or Frank's RedHot, which are used to flavor a range of dishes, such as chilis, stews, salad dressings, and Southern-style recipes.

Brown Rice and Chicken Salad with Miso Dressing

This salad is fiber-rich thanks to its use of brown rice. The process that produces brown rice removes only the hull, leaving the nutritious tan-colored bran attached. The shiro (white) miso used here is made from cooked and mashed soy beans injected and fermented with koji, a yeast-like mold, and then matured for a few months. It is lighter in color, lower in salt, and mellower and sweeter in flavor than other longer-aged miso pastes. Look for it at Japanese food stores and many supermarkets.

Prep time: 25 minutes • Cooking time: about 35 minutes • Makes: 8 servings

1 cup (250 mL) long-grain brown rice

2 cups (500 mL) cold water

5 Tbsp (75 mL) vegetable oil

2 Tbsp (30 mL) rice vinegar

1 Tbsp (15 mL) white (shiro) miso

1 Tbsp (15 mL) soy sauce

2 tsp (10 mL) honey

2 tsp (10 mL) chopped fresh ginger

1 garlic clove, minced

1 small carrot, grated

1 cup (250 mL) finely diced rotisserie chicken meat

1 medium red bell pepper, diced

⅓ medium cucumber, diced

3 green onions, thinly sliced

¾ cup (175 mL) frozen peas or edamame (green soy beans), thawed

1. Place the rice and water in a small pot and bring to a boil over high heat. Cover, reduce the heat to its lowest setting, and cook for 35 minutes, or until tender. Spoon the rice onto a wide plate and allow to cool to room temperature.

2. Place the vegetable oil, vinegar, miso, soy sauce, honey, ginger, and garlic in a large bowl and whisk until well mixed. Add in the cooked rice, carrots, chicken, bell peppers, cucumber, green onions, and peas (or edamame). Toss gently to combine, and serve family style. (You can make this salad several hours ahead, cover, and refrigerate until needed. Toss gently before serving.)

Spicy Chicken, Mango, and Cucumber Salad

This Southeast Asian–style chicken salad combines sweet, sour, and spicy flavors with bright-tasting fresh ingredients and rich nuts and chicken. To be sure the ingredients remain crisp and crunchy, make it no more than an hour ahead. Serrano peppers are very hot, so wear rubber gloves when chopping and handling this fiery pepper. Also be careful not to put your fingers near your eyes or any other sensitive area on your body.

Prep time: 30 minutes • Cooking time: none • Makes: 8 servings

¼ cup (60 mL) orange juice

2 Tbsp (30 mL) lime juice

2 Tbsp (30 mL) vegetable oil

1 cup (250 mL) diced rotisserie
   chicken meat

2 medium ripe mangoes, peeled and sliced

½ English cucumber, halved lengthwise
   and thinly sliced

1 cup (250 mL) finely chopped red bell
   peppers

½ to 1 small hot serrano chili pepper,
   halved lengthwise, seeds discarded
   and flesh finely chopped

2 medium shallots, halved lengthwise
   and thinly sliced

2 tsp (10 mL) finely grated fresh ginger

3 Tbsp (45 mL) chopped fresh mint or
   cilantro or basil

Salt to taste

⅓ cup (80 mL) unsalted roasted peanuts
   or cashews, coarsely chopped

1. Place all the ingredients in a bowl and toss to combine. Cover and refrigerate for up to 1 hour, then gently toss again before serving.

ABOUT MANGOES

Ripe juicy mangoes make a refreshing, tropical addition to any dish. An added bonus is that they contain vitamins A, B, C, and D, fiber, and potassium.

When purchasing, look for fruit that is heavy for its size and has unblemished skin. A ripe mango has a heavenly tropical-fruit aroma, and the flesh under the skin yields slightly to gentle pressure. An unripe mango can be left at room temperature for a few days or placed in a paper bag overnight to speed up the ripening process. Refrigerate ripe mangoes until ready to use.

SANDWICHES, WRAPS, AND PIZZA

Rotisserie Chicken Wraps with Grapes, Carrots, and Almonds

Healthy, delicious, and quick to prepare, these chicken-rich wraps are flecked with juicy grapes, sweet and earthy raw carrots, and crunchy almonds. That makes them a good choice for a work or school lunch, when you have leftover rotisserie chicken to use up.

Prep time: 15 minutes • Cooking time: none • Makes: 4 wraps

4 flour or whole-wheat tortillas, each
   10 inches (25 cm) in diameter

⅓ cup (80 mL) mayonnaise, or to taste

4 tsp (20 mL) Dijon mustard, or to taste

4 to 6 cups (1 to 1.5 L) baby salad greens
   or arugula or spinach

Meat from ½ a rotisserie chicken,
   thinly sliced

16 seedless red grapes, halved

½ cup (125 mL) grated carrots

⅓ cup (80 mL) unsalted whole almonds,
   skins on

1. Arrange the tortillas on a clean work surface. Spread one side of each tortilla with mayonnaise and mustard. Place a row of salad greens down the center of each tortilla, then top with the chicken, grapes, carrots, and almonds.

2. Fold the sides of each tortilla partially over the filling, then fold the bottom of the tortilla over the filling and roll into a tight cylinder. (You can make the wraps to this point, wrap them in plastic wrap, and refrigerate until lunchtime.) Cut each wrap in half widthwise and enjoy.

ABOUT ALMONDS

Almonds are native to western Asia but are now grown in other warm climates, such as the Mediterranean, Australia, and California. They are nutritionally rich and contain fiber, vitamins B and E, and calcium, potassium, and folic acid. Like other nuts, almonds are rich in fat, but almost entirely monounsaturated and polyunsaturated fat, which may help lower cholesterol levels. Because of their high fat content, almonds can go rancid fairly quickly.

Refrigerate shelled almonds in an airtight container for up to 4 months or freeze them for up to 6 months. Unshelled nuts will keep about twice as long as shelled ones.

Asian-style Chicken Bunwiches with Ginger Sauce

This delicious recipe is inspired by the popular Vietnamese-style bánh mì sandwich, which is sold at food trucks and restaurants. It's made with slices of rotisserie chicken piled into buns and flavored with crisp vegetables, cilantro, and an addictive ginger sauce. As an alternative, wrap the filling in lettuce leaves instead.

Prep time: 30 minutes • Cooking time: 5 minutes • Makes: 4 servings

Ginger sauce

⅔ cup (160 mL) mayonnaise

1 Tbsp (15 mL) finely grated fresh ginger

2 Tbsp (30 mL) soy sauce

1 Tbsp (15 mL) rice vinegar or lime juice

1 tsp (5 mL) honey, or to taste

1 tsp (5 mL) sesame oil

Bunwiches

Meat from ½ a rotisserie chicken,
   thinly sliced

⅓ cup (80 mL) chicken stock (page 59)

4 hot dog or panini buns, split and warmed

1 cup (250 mL) shredded leaf or head
   lettuce

Asian-style hot chili sauce to taste
   (page 88)

¼ cup (60 mL) grated carrots

¼ cup (60 mL) grated English cucumber

2 Tbsp (30 mL) chopped fresh cilantro

Ginger sauce

1. In a small bowl, combine all the ingredients until well mixed. Cover and refrigerate until ready to make the sandwiches. Any leftover sauce will keep refrigerated in an airtight container for up to 1 week.

Bunwiches

1. Place the chicken and stock in a skillet over medium heat, cover, and cook for 5 minutes, or until hot.

2. Generously spread the ginger sauce on the cut sides of each hot dog bun. Top with the lettuce, hot chicken, and a little more ginger sauce. Add a drizzle of hot chili sauce (if using).

3. Cover with the carrots, cucumber, and cilantro and serve.

Chicken Gyros

In Greek restaurants, gyros are usually made with sliced lamb that's been cooked on a vertical spit and wrapped in pita bread. This folded or rolled sandwich is also popular in other countries around the Mediterranean, where it is known as donair or shawarma, depending on where it comes from. In this version, though, cubes of flavorful rotisserie chicken are sandwiched in the pita with appealing accents, such as olives, feta cheese, and tzatziki. This yogurt-based sauce flavored with cucumber, garlic, and herbs is sold at just about every supermarket and Mediterranean-style food store.

Prep time: 15 minutes • Cooking time: 5 minutes • Makes: 4 servings

⅓ cup (80 mL) chicken stock (page 59)

2 tsp (10 mL) lemon juice

½ tsp (2 mL) ground cumin

½ tsp (2 mL) oregano

1 small garlic clove, minced

2 cups (500 mL) diced rotisserie chicken meat, or to taste

4 Greek-style pita breads, warmed (see Note)

½ cup (125 mL) tzatziki sauce

½ cup (125 mL) shredded lettuce

⅓ cup (80 mL) crumbled feta cheese

12 pitted black olives, halved

⅓ cup (80 mL) diced English cucumber, or to taste

8 cherry tomatoes, quartered

1. Place the stock, lemon juice, cumin, oregano, and garlic in a wide skillet and bring to a simmer over medium heat. Add the chicken, cover, and cook until the chicken is hot, about 5 minutes.

2. Arrange the pitas on individual plates. Spread ¼ of the tzatziki sauce down the center of each pita. Arrange the chicken over the tzatziki sauce.

3. Top each pita with lettuce, feta cheese, olives, cucumbers, and tomatoes.

4. Serve, and allow guests to roll or fold their own pitas.

Note: Greek-style pita, also called souvlaki pita, is a pocketless version of the popular Mediterranean bread. It's sold in the deli department of most supermarkets and at Mediterranean food stores.

Chicken, Avocado, and Tomato Melts

To make a splendid lunch or dinner, serve these sumptuous melts with a simple green salad and a glass of lemonade or iced tea.

Prep time: 15 minutes • Cooking time: 10 minutes • Makes: 4 servings

2 tsp (10 mL) lime juice

1 medium ripe avocado

4 slices French bread, each 1 inch (2.5 cm) thick

4 Tbsp (60 mL) mayonnaise

1½ cups (375 mL) baby arugula or spinach

8 slices ripe tomato

1⅓ cups (330 mL) shredded rotisserie chicken meat

1 cup (250 mL) grated plain or jalapeño-flavored Monterey Jack cheese

¼ cup (60 mL) coarsely chopped fresh cilantro or green onions

1. Preheat the oven to 425°F (220°C). Line a baking sheet with parchment paper. Pour the lime juice onto a wide plate.

2. Quarter the avocado lengthwise, pull it apart, and discard the pit. Remove the peel from the avocado. Cut each quarter piece of avocado, lengthwise, into 3 slices. Set the avocado on the plate and coat with the lime juice.

3. Spread mayonnaise on one side of each slice of bread and arrange on the baking sheet. Top each slice with arugula (or spinach), 2 slices of tomato, 3 slices of avocado, and ⅓ cup (80 mL) of the shredded chicken. Sprinkle with cheese.

4. Bake for 10 minutes, or until the cheese is melted and the bottom of the bread is lightly toasted. Garnish with cilantro (or green onions) and serve.

ABOUT AVOCADOS

Avocados are a source of potassium and vitamins C and A, and they are high in monounsaturated fat, a healthy fat that may help lower blood cholesterol levels.

When purchasing, choose avocados that feel heavy for their size and are free of dark, sunken spots. Ripe and ready-to-eat avocados will feel slightly soft when gently squeezed.

To ripen hard avocados, simply leave them at room temperature for a few days. To speed up the ripening process, place them in a brown paper bag. Conversely, if you have ripe avocados and don't need them right away, refrigerate and use them within 2 to 3 days to prevent them from over-ripening.

A quick way to peel an avocado is to cut it lengthwise into quarters and pull each quarter away from the pit. Pull the skin off each quarter with a paring knife and use the flesh as desired. Avocado flesh darkens quickly when exposed to air. To help prevent that, brush or toss any cut surfaces with lime or lemon juice.

Grilled Chicken, Gouda, and Apple Sandwiches

Melted cheese can make anything taste good! Here, sumptuous chicken is combined with tangy cheese and sweet apple in these tasty hot sandwiches.

Prep time: 10 minutes • Cooking time: 6 to 8 minutes • Makes: 2 sandwiches

2 Tbsp (30 mL) butter, room temperature

4 slices white, whole-wheat, or sour-dough bread

2 Tbsp (30 mL) mayonnaise

2 tsp (10 mL) Dijon mustard

½ to ¾ cup (125 to 175 mL) thinly sliced rotisserie chicken meat

1 small unpeeled green or red apple, cored, quartered, and thinly sliced

1 cup (250 mL) grated Gouda or Gruyère or aged cheddar cheese

1. Butter one side of each slice of bread. Spread mayonnaise and mustard on the unbuttered side of 2 of those slices. Top with the chicken, apples, cheese, and the remaining slices of bread, buttered side up.

2. Heat a large nonstick skillet over medium-low to medium heat. Place the sandwiches in the pan and cook for 3 to 4 minutes per side, or until the cheese is melted and the bread is nicely toasted. Slice the sandwiches in halves or quarters and serve.

Chicken Reuben Sandwiches with Russian Dressing

This deluxe version of a traditional Reuben sandwich layers chicken instead of the usual corned beef with two types of cheese, sauerkraut, and a zesty dressing.

Prep time: 15 minutes • Cooking time: 8 to 10 minutes • Makes: 2 sandwiches

Russian dressing

⅓ cup (80 mL) mayonnaise

2 Tbsp (30 mL) finely chopped sweet
   mixed pickles

1 Tbsp (15 mL) ketchup

⅛ tsp (0.5 mL) paprika

Splashes of Worcestershire sauce and
   red wine vinegar

Freshly ground black pepper to taste

Reuben sandwiches

1 Tbsp (15 mL) butter, room temperature

4 slices dark rye, sourdough, or French
   bread

½ cup (125 mL) grated Swiss cheese

½ cup (125 mL) grated Gouda cheese

1 cup (250 mL) thinly sliced rotisserie
   chicken meat

¾ cup (175 mL) well-drained sauerkraut

Russian dressing

1. In a small bowl, combine all the ingredients until well mixed. Cover and refrigerate until needed.

Reuben sandwiches

1. Lightly butter one side of each slice of bread. Spread Russian dressing on the unbuttered side of 2 of those slices. (Refrigerate any leftover dressing for another use.) Top with ½ of the cheese, chicken, and sauerkraut. Finish with the remaining cheese and the remaining slices of bread, buttered side up.

2. Heat a nonstick skillet over medium-low to medium heat. Add the sandwiches and grill for 4 to 5 minutes per side, or until the cheese is melted and the sauerkraut and chicken are heated through. Cut each sandwich in half and enjoy.

Pulled Chicken Sliders

Tired of beef or pulled pork sliders? These chicken sliders are made by warming shreds of rotisserie chicken in a barbecue sauce mixture and piling them into mini hamburger buns. Chipotle peppers are smoked jalapeño peppers. They are sold in cans at most supermarkets. Try these sliders with Sweet and Sour Coleslaw with Cranberries and Apricots (page 152) or Miniature Potato Salad with Grainy Dijon and Chives (page 158).

Prep time: 20 minutes • Cooking time: about 10 minutes • Makes: 6 servings (2 sliders each)

1 rotisserie chicken

1 cup (250 mL) regular or flavored barbecue sauce

⅓ cup (80 mL) apple juice

2 Tbsp (30 mL) cider vinegar

1 tsp (5 mL) hot pepper sauce, such as Tabasco

1 tsp (5 mL) Worcestershire sauce

1 chipotle pepper, finely sliced (optional)

12 small lettuce leaves

12 slider (mini hamburger) buns

12 small slices onion

12 slices bread-and-butter pickles

1. With your fingers, remove and discard the skin from the chicken, and then pull off the meat. Using your fingers, pull that meat into 1-inch (2.5 cm) shreds and set in a bowl.

2. Place the barbecue sauce, apple juice, vinegar, hot pepper sauce, Worcestershire sauce, and chipotle pepper (if using) in a wide skillet and bring to a simmer over medium heat. Stir in the shredded chicken and cook for 7 to 10 minutes, or until the chicken is hot.

3. Arrange a lettuce leaf on the bottom half of each bun. Top with a mound of chicken, a slice of onion, a slice of pickle, and the top half of the bun. Serve immediately, and enjoy.

Open-faced Hot Chicken Sandwiches with Onion Gravy

On a cold and rainy day, nothing beats a mound of hot rotisserie chicken meat simmered in gravy and heaped on fresh bread. For a diner-style meal, serve these sandwiches with French fries and Sweet and Sour Coleslaw with Cranberries and Apricots (page 152).

Prep time: 15 minutes • Cooking time: about 15 minutes • Makes: 6 servings

3 Tbsp (45 mL) butter or vegetable oil

1 small onion, finely chopped

3 Tbsp (45 mL) all-purpose flour

2½ cups (625 mL) chicken stock (page 59)

1 rotisserie chicken, meat removed and sliced

Salt and freshly ground black pepper to taste

6 slices whole-wheat or white bread

2 green onions, thinly sliced (optional)

1. Melt the butter (or heat the vegetable oil) in a large skillet over medium heat. Add the onions and cook until softened, 4 to 5 minutes.

2. Stir in the flour and cook for 2 to 3 minutes, until this roux you have created is lightly browned. Slowly whisk in the stock and bring to a simmer. Add the chicken, season lightly with salt and pepper, and cook for 5 minutes, or until the chicken is hot.

3. Arrange the bread on individual plates. Mound the chicken on the bread, spoon gravy over top, sprinkle with green onions (if using), and serve.

ABOUT ROUX

Roux is a mixture of butter (or oil or animal fat) and flour in equal proportions that is cooked before it's combined with the liquid it will be used to thicken, such as stock or milk. For a light-colored, milk-based white sauce, such as a béchamel sauce, the roux is cooked only a minute or so to eliminate the taste of uncooked flour. For a chicken gravy or a darker sauce, the roux can be cooked until it is light or dark brown before adding the liquid.

No-fuss Rotisserie Chicken Enchiladas

Supermarket conveniences, such as precooked rotisserie chicken, bottled salsa, and canned refried beans, make these enchiladas easy to prepare. Serve with Spanish-style Rice (page 177).

Prep time: 25 minutes • Cooking time: 25 to 30 minutes • Makes: 6 servings

2 cups (500 mL) storebought tomato salsa

½ cup (125 mL) chicken stock (page 59)

1 rotisserie chicken

2 cups (500 mL) grated Monterey Jack cheese, divided

1 can (14 oz/398 mL) refried beans

6 flour tortillas, each 10 inches (25 cm) in diameter

¼ cup (60 mL) chopped fresh cilantro or thinly sliced green onions

¾ cup (175 mL) sour cream, or to taste

1. Preheat the oven to 375°F (190°C). Line a large baking sheet with parchment paper.

2. Combine the salsa and stock in a medium bowl.

3. With your fingers, remove and discard the skin from the chicken, and then pull off the meat. Using your fingers, pull that meat into 1-inch (2.5 cm) shreds and set in a second, larger bowl. Add half of the salsa/stock mixture and half of the cheese, and toss to combine.

4. Spread the refried beans along the center of each tortilla. Top with an equal amount of the chicken mixture. Fold the bottom half of the tortilla over the filling, then roll each tortilla into a cylinder. Arrange the tortillas on the prepared baking sheet, about 2 inches (5 cm) apart.

5. Spoon the remaining salsa evenly over the tortillas and sprinkle with the remaining cheese. Bake, uncovered, for 25 to 30 minutes, or until the cheese is melted and golden and the enchiladas have heated through.

6. Serve the enchiladas on individual plates, sprinkle with cilantro (or green onions), and serve with a dollop of sour cream.

Polenta Pizza with Chicken, Olives, Fennel, and Asiago

Polenta is a cooked, thick cornmeal mixture that, when spread on a pizza pan and baked, provides a dense, wheat-free crust.

Prep time: 25 minutes, plus cooling and setting • Cooking time: 32 to 37 minutes • Makes: 4 servings (2 wedges each)

1 Tbsp (15 mL) olive oil

3½ cups (875 mL) water

1 tsp (5 mL) salt

1 cup (250 mL) cornmeal

½ cup (125 mL) tomato sauce

1 cup (250 mL) grated asiago cheese

1 cup (250 mL) shredded rotisserie chicken meat, or to taste

8 to 12 pitted black olives, halved

¼ tsp (1 mL) fennel seeds, coarsely crushed

8 to 12 fresh basil leaves

1. Brush a 12-inch (30 cm) nonstick pizza pan with the olive oil and set aside.

2. Pour the water into a medium, heavy-bottomed pot and bring to a boil over medium-high heat. Add the salt, and then reduce the heat to medium. While whisking steadily, slowly pour in the cornmeal. Reduce the heat to medium-low and cook for 5 minutes, whisking frequently.

3. Using a sturdy wooden spoon to stir the polenta, cook, stirring frequently, for 15 minutes more. At this point the polenta will be quite thick but spreadable.

4. Spoon the polenta onto the prepared pizza pan and quickly spread into a circle ¼ to ½ inch (6 mm to 1.25 cm) thick. Allow to cool to room temperature and set, about 20 minutes. (Polenta pizza can be made to this point several hours in advance; cover and refrigerate until ready to top and bake.)

5. Preheat the oven to 450°F (230°C). Evenly spread tomato sauce over the polenta. Top with the cheese, chicken, and olives. Sprinkle with the fennel seeds. Bake for 12 to 15 minutes, until the polenta is hot and a little crispy on the bottom.

6. Remove from the oven and allow to cool for 3 to 4 minutes. Top with fresh basil, cut in 8 wedges, and serve.

PASTA, RICE, AND ASIAN NOODLES

Rotini with Chicken, Cauliflower, Arugula, and Prosciutto

Savor the flavors of Italy with this corkscrew-shaped pasta tossed with chicken and vegetables and a modest amount of flavor-enhancing prosciutto.

Prep time: 15 minutes • Cooking time: about 20 minutes • Makes: 4 servings

30 thumb-size cauliflower florets (about 10 oz/300 g)

¾ lb (375 g) rotini or penne

3 Tbsp (45 mL) olive oil

2 cups (500 mL) loosely packed baby arugula or kale or spinach

1 cup (250 mL) diced rotisserie chicken meat

3 thin slices prosciutto, coarsely chopped

1 large garlic clove, minced

Pinches of dried oregano and crushed chili flakes

¾ cup (175 mL) chicken stock (page 59)

⅓ cup (80 mL) freshly grated parmesan cheese

1. Fill a bowl with ice-cold water. Bring a large pot of water to a boil over medium-high heat. Add the cauliflower and cook until just tender, about 3 minutes.

2. Using a slotted spoon, transfer the cauliflower to the ice-cold water, drain well, and set on a plate. Reserve the pot of boiling water.

3. Add the rotini to the pot of boiling water and cook until tender, 8 to 10 minutes.

4. While the pasta is cooking, heat the olive oil in a very large, wide skillet over medium to medium-high heat. Add the cauliflower, arugula (or kale or spinach), chicken, prosciutto, garlic, oregano, and chili flakes and cook, stirring, for 3 to 4 minutes, until the arugula has wilted and the cauliflower is lightly colored. Pour in the stock and allow to come to a simmer.

5. Drain the pasta well, reserving ½ cup (125 mL) of its cooking liquid.

6. Stir the pasta, reserved cooking liquid, and cheese into the chicken/vegetable mixture, toss to combine, and serve.

Rich and Creamy Pasta Alfredo with Chicken

This rich, garlicky, creamy pasta is studded with bits of rotisserie chicken not usually found in this popular dish. That addition provides added protein, flavor, and even more richness.

Prep time: 10 minutes • Cooking time: 10 minutes • Makes: 4 servings

¾ lb (375 g) bowtie, rotini, or other pasta

1½ cups (375 mL) whipping cream

1½ cups (375 mL) diced rotisserie chicken meat

2 large garlic cloves, minced

½ tsp (2 mL) dried oregano

Salt and freshly ground black pepper to taste

⅓ cup (80 mL) freshly grated parmesan cheese + more for sprinkling

1 to 2 Tbsp (15 to 30 mL) chopped fresh parsley

1. Bring a large pot of lightly salted water to a boil over medium-high heat. Add the pasta and cook until just tender, 8 to 10 minutes.

2. While the pasta is cooking, place the cream, chicken, garlic, and oregano in a skillet over medium heat. Bring to a simmer, season with salt and pepper, and reduce the heat to low.

3. Drain the pasta well, reserving ½ cup (125 mL) of its cooking liquid.

4. Stir the pasta, reserved cooking liquid, ⅓ cup (80 mL) of parmesan, and parsley into the chicken mixture and toss well.

5. Divide the pasta among individual bowls and serve immediately. Sprinkle with additional parmesan cheese, if desired.

HOW TO COOK PASTA

Be generous with the water. For each ¾ to 1 lb (375 to 500 g) of pasta, bring at least 12 cups (3 L) of water to a boil in a deep pot. Using lots of water prevents the pasta from sticking together as it cooks, and using a deep pot makes it easier to submerge long pasta, such as spaghetti.

Hold off on the oil. Many people add oil to the cooking water to prevent the pasta from sticking as it cooks. But if you use lots of water, there's no need for oil. In fact, adding oil makes the pasta slick, which prevents tasty sauces from clinging to it.

Do add salt. Plain pasta is not seasoned, so add 2 to 3 tsp (10 to 15 mL) of salt for every 12 cups (3 L) of water. As the pasta cooks, it absorbs the salt, which contributes to the overall flavor of the dish.

Cook until al dente (in Italian, "to the bite"). When properly cooked, the pasta should resist slightly when you bite into it, but the center should not be hard or uncooked. Check the package for the suggested cooking time, and taste the pasta while it's cooking to see how it's progressing.

Creamy Chicken and Squash Lasagna

This-perfect-for-autumn casserole layers earthy squash, bits of chicken, noodles, cheese, spinach, and a creamy sauce. Pair it with a simple green salad and Focaccia Bread with Herbs and Onions (page 190).

Prep time: 30 minutes • Cooking time: about 80 minutes • Makes: 8 servings

5 cups (1.25 L) peeled, cubed banana or butternut or hubbard squash

Salt and white pepper to taste

2 medium garlic cloves, minced

1 tsp (5 mL) dried sage leaves

1 cup (250 mL) light cream

2¼ cups (560 mL) milk, divided

¼ cup (60 mL) all-purpose flour

¼ tsp (1 mL) grated nutmeg

2 cups (500 mL) diced rotisserie chicken meat, divided

1 lb (500 g) mozzarella cheese, grated, divided

16 dry lasagna noodles, cooked and cooled

2 cups (500 mL) fresh baby spinach

1. Place the squash in a large pot, cover with water, and boil over medium-high heat until tender, 8 to 10 minutes. Drain well, return to the pot, and mash. Season with salt and pepper and set aside.

2. Combine the garlic, sage, cream, and 1¾ cups (425 mL) of the milk in a large pot over medium heat.

3. When the cream mixture is barely simmering, pour the remaining ½ cup (125 mL) of milk into a bowl, gradually add the flour, and whisk until smooth. Whisk this mixture into the simmering cream and cook until slightly thickened. Remove from the heat and stir in the nutmeg.

4. Preheat the oven to 350°F (180°C). Have ready a deep 9- × 13-inch (3.5 L) baking dish.

5. To assemble, spoon ½ cup (125 mL) of the cream sauce into the baking dish, spreading it evenly. Top with 4 noodles, ¾ cup (175 mL) of the sauce, and ½ the squash. Sprinkle ½ of the chicken over the squash. Top with ¼ of the cheese.

6. Place 4 more noodles over the cheese and top with ¾ cup (175 mL) of the sauce. Sprinkle with the spinach and another ¼ of the cheese.

7. Repeat the layering of noodles, cheese, and sauce, and top with the remaining squash and chicken. Sprinkle with ¼ of the cheese and the remaining noodles. Spread the last of the sauce over the noodles and sprinkle with the remaining cheese.

8. Cover with aluminum foil and bake for 40 minutes. Remove the foil and bake for 10 to 15 minutes more, or until the cheese is golden and bubbly. Allow to rest for 10 minutes before cutting and serving.

Mac and Cheese with Chicken and Peas

Make a filling meal of this classic comfort food by serving it with Dinner Buns (page 182) and a green salad, such as Leaf Lettuce Salad with Ranch Dressing, Bacon Bits, and Tomatoes (page 150). Use whole-wheat pasta, if you prefer.

Prep time: 20 to 25 minutes • Cooking time: about 40 minutes • Makes: 6 servings

2 cups (500 mL) macaroni

3 Tbsp (45 mL) butter + more for greasing

3 Tbsp (45 mL) all-purpose flour

2½ cups (625 mL) warm milk (see Note), divided

¼ tsp (1 mL) paprika

Pinch of cayenne pepper

Salt and white pepper to taste

2 cups (500 mL) grated cheddar cheese, divided

1 cup (250 mL) diced rotisserie chicken meat

½ cup (125 mL) frozen peas

2 to 3 Tbsp (30 to 45 mL) freshly grated parmesan cheese

Note: Warm milk in a small heat-proof bowl by placing it in the microwave. Heat on high, in 1-minute spurts, until heated to just below a simmer.

1. Bring a large pot of lightly salted water to a boil over medium-high heat. Add the macaroni and cook until just tender, about 8 minutes.

2. While the macaroni cooks, preheat the oven to 350°F (180°C). Lightly grease an 8-inch (20 cm) square baking dish.

3. Melt the butter in a pot over medium heat. Mix in the flour and cook, stirring, for 2 minutes. Using a whisk, slowly incorporate ½ cup (125 mL) of the milk into the flour mixture, stirring constantly until the mixture is quite thick, about 1 minute. Slowly whisk in the remaining milk and bring to a simmer, stirring frequently, for 1 minute, until thick. Remove the sauce from the heat, then mix in the paprika, cayenne, salt, pepper, and ¾ of the cheddar cheese.

4. Drain the macaroni well and gently fold into the cheese sauce. Stir in the chicken and peas, then spoon the mixture into the baking dish. Top with the remaining cheddar and the parmesan. Bake for 25 to 30 minutes, or until the macaroni is golden on top and deliciously hot.

Simple and Hearty Chicken Stew on Egg Noodles

Serve this easy-to-make, rotisserie-chicken-based stew with Flaky Buttermilk Biscuits (page 184). Use broad European-style egg noodles in this dish.

Prep time: 20 minutes • Cooking time: about 30 minutes • Makes: 3 to 4 servings

3 Tbsp (45 mL) vegetable oil

½ large onion, cut in ½-inch (1.25 cm) cubes

1 medium carrot, cut in ½-inch (1.25 cm) cubes

1 medium celery stalk, cut in ½-inch (1.25 cm) cubes

3 Tbsp (45 mL) all-purpose flour

Pinches of dried sage leaves and paprika

1 Tbsp (15 mL) Dijon mustard

3½ cups (875 mL) chicken stock (page 59), divided

2 cups (500 mL) rotisserie chicken meat, cut in ¾- to 1-inch (2 to 2.5 cm) cubes

Splash or 2 of Worcestershire sauce

½ cup (125 mL) frozen peas or corn, or a mix of both

1 bag (11 oz/350 g) broad egg noodles

¼ cup (60 mL) whipping cream (optional)

Salt and freshly ground black pepper to taste

1. Heat the vegetable oil in a 10-inch (25 cm) wide, heavy-bottomed pot over medium to medium-high heat. Add the onions, carrots, and celery and cook until softened, 4 to 5 minutes.

2. Stir in the flour, sage, paprika, and mustard and cook for 2 minutes more. Slowly add ½ cup (125 mL) of the stock, stirring constantly. Cook for 1 minute or so, and when the mixture is very thick, slowly mix in the remaining stock.

3. Add the chicken and Worcestershire sauce, bring the stew to a gentle simmer, and cook, uncovered, for 20 minutes, until lightly thickened and richly flavored.

4. While the stew simmers, set a large pot of water over medium-high heat and bring it to a boil. Add the egg noodles and cook until tender, about 5 minutes. Drain well.

5. Add the peas and/or corn and cream (if using) to the stew and cook for 2 minutes more, until heated through. Season with salt and pepper.

6. To serve, divide the noodles among 3 to 4 shallow bowls. Make a well in the middle and spoon the stew into the center.

Rotisserie Chicken on Mixed-Mushroom Risotto

The best rice for risotto is a stubby, short- or medium-grained variety with a high starch content. It absorbs less liquid as it cooks than other varieties, with the result that an almost creamy sauce forms around the grains. This is the key to delicious risotto. Look for arborio, carnaroli, or vialone nano varieties, or for products simply labeled as "Italian rice."

Prep time: 40 minutes • Cooking time: about 30 minutes • Makes: 4 servings

3 Tbsp (45 mL) olive oil, divided

¼ lb (125 g) white mushrooms, sliced

¼ lb (125 g) brown mushrooms, sliced

¼ lb (125 g) oyster mushrooms, sliced (see Note)

1 medium onion, finely chopped

1½ cups (375 mL) arborio, carnaroli, vialone nano, or other risotto rice

½ cup (125 mL) white wine (or chicken stock)

1 medium garlic clove, minced

1 tsp (5 mL) dried oregano

6 cups (1.5 L) chicken stock (page 59), hot

½ cup (125 mL) freshly grated parmesan cheese + more for sprinkling

Salt and freshly ground black pepper to taste

1 rotisserie chicken, hot, cut into portions (page 16)

1 Tbsp (15 mL) chopped fresh parsley

1. Heat 1 Tbsp (15 mL) of the olive oil in a large skillet over medium or medium-high heat. Add the mushrooms and cook until they release their juices and become tender, 5 to 6 minutes. Remove from the heat and set aside.

2. Heat the remaining 2 Tbsp (30 mL) of olive oil in a medium, heavy-bottomed pot over medium heat. Add the onions and cook until softened, about 4 minutes.

3. Stir in the rice and cook, stirring, until it achieves a nutty, toasted aroma, 2 to 3 minutes.

4. Add the ½ cup (125 mL) of wine (or chicken stock), garlic, and oregano, and reduce the heat until the wine simmers gently. Cook until the wine is almost fully absorbed, 3 to 4 minutes.

5. Add 1 cup (250 mL) of hot stock, stirring until it is almost fully absorbed. Add the remaining stock, 1 cup (250 mL) at a time, stirring after each addition until it is almost fully absorbed. Continue adding stock and stirring until the rice is tender. (You may not need all the stock.)

6. Mix in the reserved mushrooms, parmesan, and salt and pepper. Turn off the heat and allow to stand for 5 minutes.

7. Divide the risotto among 4 shallow bowls. Top with the chicken, sprinkle with parsley, and serve.

Note: The lower part of an oyster mushroom's stem is tough, so trim it away before slicing the mushroom.

Shrimp and Chicken Paella with Chorizo and Olives

Paella originated in Valencia, Spain, and the traditional dish draws on ingredients from that region, including meat and poultry, seafood, beans, tomatoes, and saffron. These days, cooks the world over prepare paella with their own local ingredients.

Prep time: about 30 minutes, plus steeping time • Cooking time: about 30 minutes • Makes: 4 servings

½ tsp (2 mL) saffron threads (page 120)

2 Tbsp (30 mL) hot water

12 to 16 medium to large shrimp, unpeeled

2 fresh chorizo sausages, each about 2½ oz (75 g)

2 Tbsp (30 mL) olive oil

½ medium onion, finely chopped

½ medium green bell pepper, finely chopped

1 large garlic clove, minced

8 cherry tomatoes, quartered

1½ cups (375 mL) long-grain white rice

½ tsp (2 mL) dried oregano

3 cups (750 mL) chicken stock (page 59) + more as needed

Freshly ground black pepper to taste

1 to 1½ cups (250 to 375 mL) cubed rotisserie chicken meat

16 unpitted black or green olives, or a mix of both

¼ cup (60 mL) frozen peas

4 lemon wedges, for garnish

1. Crumble the saffron threads into a small bowl, add the hot water, and allow to steep for 30 minutes.

2. While the saffron is steeping, use kitchen scissors to make a slit lengthwise along the back of each shrimp (this will make them easier to peel and eat once they've been cooked in the paella). Thoroughly rinse the shrimp under cold running water, then pat dry with paper towels. Set aside on a plate, cover, and refrigerate until needed.

3. Squeeze the sausage meat from its casings into a small bowl. Discard the casings. Using your fingers, pull the sausage meat into pieces ¼ to ½ inch (6 mm to 1.25 cm) long.

4. Heat the olive oil in a large skillet or paella pan over medium to medium-high heat. Add the sausage and stir until just cooked through, about 5 minutes.

5. Add the onions and bell peppers and cook until tender, about 5 minutes. Stir in the garlic, tomatoes, rice, and oregano and cook for 2 minutes more.

6. Pour in the chicken stock and saffron and its liquid. Season with black pepper, and then bring to a boil, cover, and reduce the heat to medium-low. Cook for 10 minutes.

cont'd overleaf

7. Remove the lid and arrange the shrimp, chicken, and olives on top of the rice, gently pushing and nestling them into the rice. (Add a little more stock to the pan if the rice is looking overly dry.) Cover and cook for 8 to 10 minutes more, or until the shrimp are cooked and the rice is tender.

8. Sprinkle the peas into the pan, and allow them to thaw and heat through for 1 to 2 minutes. Garnish the paella with lemon wedges, then set the pan on a trivet on the dining table along with some serving plates. Dig in.

ABOUT SAFFRON THREADS

Saffron threads are the handpicked and dried stigmas of the Crocus sativa plant, which is why they are so expensive. It is worth seeking them out, however, for their slightly bitter/sweet—some say honey-like—flavor and vivid red color. The best-quality stigmas are brittle yet intact, are uniform in color, and have a strong, fresh, almost hay-like aroma. A musty scent is a sign the saffron is old or has been improperly dried or stored. Saffron is available, often in small bottles, plastic boxes, or envelopes, in the spice aisle of some supermarkets. You'll also find it for sale at specialty food stores.

Curry-spiced Jasmine Fried Rice with Chicken

Jasmine rice is sold in bags in the rice aisle of most supermarkets. It is a long-grained variety with a splendidly aromatic jasmine flower–like scent, hence its name. In this recipe, the rice is fried with curry powder, turning it a striking gold color and infusing it with a spicy taste. The rice is also complemented with bits of chicken, vegetables, mushrooms, and water chestnuts. Before you start cooking, see About fried rice.

Prep time: 20 minutes • Cooking time: 8 minutes • Makes: 6 servings

2 Tbsp (30 mL) vegetable oil

½ medium onion, finely chopped

½ red bell pepper, finely chopped

1 small carrot, grated

6 medium fresh shiitake mushrooms, stems removed and caps thinly sliced, or 6 white or brown mushrooms, sliced

2 tsp (10 mL) mild or medium curry powder

1 can (8 oz/250 mL) sliced water chestnuts, drained well

3 baby bok choy, trimmed, washed, and chopped

1 cup (250 mL) diced rotisserie chicken meat

4 cups (1 L) cooked jasmine rice, cold

½ cup (125 mL) chicken stock (page 59)

3 green onions, thinly sliced

1. Heat the vegetable oil in a wok or a large skillet over medium-high heat. Add the onions, bell peppers, carrots, and mushrooms and stir-fry for 3 minutes.

2. Stir in the curry powder and stir-fry for 1 minute more. Mix in the water chestnuts and bok choy and stir-fry for another minute.

3. Add the chicken, rice, stock, and green onions and cook for 3 minutes more, or until the rice is piping hot. Toss well and serve immediately.

ABOUT FRIED RICE

Use cold, cooked rice. Hot steamed rice will overcook when fried, becoming unappealingly soft. Cooled rice grains retain their shape when fried. The fried rice recipes in this book call for 4 cups (1 L) of cold cooked rice.

To cook this quantity, combine 1½ cups (375 mL) of rice and 2¼ cups (560 mL) of cold water in a small to medium pot. Bring the rice to a boil over high heat, reduce the heat to low, cover, and steam undisturbed for 15 to 18 minutes, or until just tender. Spoon the rice into a wide, shallow dish; fluff with a fork; allow to cool to room temperature; and cover and refrigerate for at least 4 hours, or overnight.

To use, allow the cooked rice to come to room temperature for 20 minutes so the grains separate easily when fried. Make sure the wok or skillet and oil are hot before you add the rice.

Chicken and Seven-Vegetable Fried Rice

Make sure you have all your ingredients chopped, measured, and ready to go before starting this quick-cooking rice dish. Before you begin, see About fried rice (page 121) and How to stir-fry (page 138).

Prep time: 20 minutes • Cooking time: about 9 minutes • Makes: 4 to 6 servings

2 Tbsp (30 mL) vegetable oil

½ medium onion, finely chopped

½ medium green bell pepper, finely chopped

1 large celery stalk, finely chopped

1 small carrot, grated

1 medium garlic clove, minced

2 tsp (10 mL) chopped fresh ginger

1 cup (250 mL) diced rotisserie chicken meat

4 cups (1 L) cooked long-grain white rice, cold

½ cup (125 mL) unsalted roasted cashews (optional)

½ cup (125 mL) frozen peas

2 green onions, thinly sliced

2 Tbsp (30 mL) light soy sauce

Freshly ground black pepper to taste

1. Heat the vegetable oil in a wok or a very large skillet over medium-high heat. Add the onions, bell peppers, celery, carrots, garlic, and ginger and stir-fry until the vegetables are just tender, 3 to 4 minutes.

2. Add the chicken, rice, and cashews and stir-fry for 2 to 3 minutes more.

3. Stir in the peas and green onions, season with soy sauce and pepper, and cook for 1 to 2 minutes more, or until piping hot. Serve immediately.

Chicken Pad Thai

This is my version of a popular noodle dish served as a street food in Thailand, and at countless Thai restaurants in North America and around the world. The combination of peanuts, soy, hot chilies, tofu, chicken, and tender noodles is hard to resist. Make this recipe as spicy as you like by adding a little, or a lot, of hot chili sauce.

Prep time: 20 minutes • Cooking time: about 6 minutes • Makes: 3 to 4 servings

¼ cup (60 mL) soy sauce

¼ cup (60 mL) brown sugar

¼ cup (60 mL) lime juice

¼ cup (60 mL) water or vegetable stock

2 Tbsp (30 mL) smooth peanut butter

2 tsp (10 mL) sesame oil

Asian-style hot chili sauce to taste
  (page 88)

2 Tbsp (30 mL) vegetable oil

1 medium onion, finely diced

1 garlic clove, minced

1 cup (250 mL) thinly shredded rotisserie
  chicken meat

6 oz (175 g) extra-firm tofu, cut in small
  cubes

8 oz (250 g) dried Asian-style rice
  noodles (see Note)

3 green onions, cut in 1-inch (2.5 cm)
  pieces

1 cup (250 mL) bean sprouts

¼ cup (60 mL) unsalted roasted peanuts,
  crushed or coarsely chopped

Sprigs of fresh cilantro and lime slices,
  for garnish

1. Bring a large pot of water to a boil over high heat. Reduce the heat to medium-high and allow the water to maintain a rolling boil.

2. In a small bowl, using a whisk, mix the soy sauce, sugar, lime juice, water (or stock), peanut butter, sesame oil, and chili sauce until well combined but not necessarily smooth. Set aside.

3. Heat the vegetable oil in a large wok or a skillet over medium-high heat. Add the onions, garlic, chicken, and tofu, and then stir-fry for 3 to 4 minutes.

4. While the wok ingredients are cooking, cook the noodles in the boiling water for 60 seconds, or until tender. Drain well.

5. Add the soy-peanut sauce to the wok and allow to come to a simmer. Add the noodles and green onions and toss to combine.

6. Divide the pad thai among individual bowls. Top with the bean sprouts and peanuts. Garnish with cilantro and lime, and serve.

Note: Dried Asian-style rice noodles are sold in the ethnic food aisle of most supermarkets and at Asian food stores. Look for the thicker fettuccine-type of noodle rather than the thin rice stick or vermicelli varieties. Uncooked leftover noodles will keep, wrapped in their original packaging, for many months.

Vietnamese-style Chicken and Rice Noodle Bowl

This is a version of the cold rice noodle bowls offered on menus at some Vietnamese restaurants. Those noodles are often topped with slices of grilled pork and fried spring rolls. In this take on the dish, a colorful mix of raw vegetables and hot pieces of rotisserie chicken take their place. Drizzle the noodles with nuoc cham, a hot, salty, and sour Vietnamese-style sauce, just before serving.

Prep time: 30 minutes • Cooking time: about 15 minutes • Makes: 4 servings

Nuoc cham

1 cup (250 mL) hot water

⅓ cup (80 mL) granulated sugar

½ tsp (2 mL) dried, crushed chili flakes

1 large garlic clove, minced

¼ cup (60 mL) fish sauce

¼ cup (60 mL) lime juice

½ cup (125 mL) grated carrots

Noodle bowl

½ lb (250 g) thin dried rice noodles (page 123)

2 cups (500 mL) shredded head or romaine lettuce

2 cups (500 mL) bean sprouts

¼ English cucumber, cut in matchstick-size slices

24 small sprigs of fresh cilantro or mint or basil

1 rotisserie chicken, hot, cut into portions (page 16)

¼ cup (60 mL) unsalted roasted peanuts, coarsely chopped, for garnish

Nuoc cham

1. Place the hot water and sugar in a medium bowl and stir until the sugar is dissolved. Stir in the chili flakes, garlic, fish sauce, lime juice, and carrots. Allow the sauce to steep for at least 15 minutes before serving. The sauce can be made a couple of hours ahead, then covered and refrigerated until needed.

Noodle bowl

1. Bring a large pot of water to a boil over medium-high heat. Add the noodles and cook for 1 minute, until just tender.

2. Drain the noodles well, and then run cold water into the pot to cool the noodles. Drain the noodles again and divide them among 4 large, shallow bowls.

3. Placing each of the ingredients in separate mounds, top the noodles with lettuce, bean sprouts, cucumber, and cilantro (or mint or basil), leaving a space on one side of the bowl for the chicken. Arrange the chicken portions in that space.

4. Sprinkle each serving with peanuts. Serve the nuoc cham in individual bowls for drizzling.

ENTRÉES

Middle Eastern–style Meal in a Bowl

Layering ingredients in a bowl has become a popular way to create a meal. The idea is that you start with a grain, add cooked or raw vegetables and/or a pulse, and follow with a protein. On goes a complementary garnish and a sauce or dressing. This version combines couscous, quinoa, or freekeh with chickpeas, spinach, tomatoes, pistachios, and a mint-orange yogurt sauce. Rotisserie chicken provides additional protein.

Prep time: 25 minutes • Cooking time: 15 to 20 minutes (to cook the grains) • Makes: 2 servings

Mint-orange yogurt sauce

⅓ cup (80 mL) plain thick yogurt

2 Tbsp (30 mL) orange juice

1 Tbsp (15 mL) chopped fresh mint

1 tsp (5 mL) honey

¼ tsp (1 mL) ground cumin

Salt and freshly ground black pepper
   to taste

Middle Eastern bowl

1 to 1½ cups (250 to 375 mL) cooked
   couscous, quinoa, or freekeh (see
   Note), cold

½ cup (125 mL) canned chickpeas,
   drained well

1 cup (250 mL) packed baby spinach

6 to 8 cherry tomatoes, halved

½ cup (125 mL) thinly sliced red or sweet
   onions

1 cup (250 mL) cooked shredded rotisserie
   chicken meat

2 Tbsp (30 mL) unsalted, shelled pistachios

¼ cup (60 mL) crumbled feta cheese

8 to 10 fresh mint leaves

Mint-orange yogurt sauce

1. In a small bowl or glass jar, combine all ingredients until well mixed. This sauce can be made several hours ahead, covered, and refrigerated until needed.

Middle Eastern bowl

1. Divide the couscous (or quinoa or freekeh) between 2 shallow bowls. Top with the chickpeas, spinach, tomatoes, and onions.

2. Arrange an equal amount of chicken in each bowl, then sprinkle with the pistachios, feta, and mint.

3. Drizzle each bowl with mint-orange yogurt sauce and enjoy.

Note: Freekeh is wheat that is harvested while it's still green, roasted, and then dried. Sold as whole grains or cracked, it is smoky and nutty and full of vitamins and minerals. Look for it in health food stores, Middle Eastern groceries, and whole-food markets, and use it as you would rice.

Creamy Chicken and Mushrooms on Polenta with Cheese

When you want to impress guests with a dish that tastes spectacular but is easy to make, pull out this recipe. Ready-to-bake polenta (see Note) saves time and soaks up a creamy sauce of mushrooms, garlic, and wine laced with bits of rotisserie chicken. Finish the dish with nuggets of cheese.

Prep time: 20 minutes • Cooking time: 20 minutes • Makes: 4 servings

1½-lb (750 g) tube of cooked polenta, cut into 12 rounds (see Note)

3 Tbsp (45 mL) olive oil, divided

2 Tbsp (30 mL) freshly grated parmesan cheese, or to taste

1 lb (500 g) assorted mushrooms, such as white, brown, oyster, and/or shiitake, tough stems removed and discarded, sliced

1 large garlic clove, minced

⅓ cup (80 mL) white wine

1 tsp (5 mL) dried tarragon

1½ cups (375 mL) whipping cream

1½ cups (375 mL) shredded rotisserie chicken meat

Salt and freshly ground black pepper

3½ oz (100 g) blue cheese or soft goat cheese, pulled into small nuggets

1 Tbsp (15 mL) chopped fresh parsley

1. Preheat the oven to 350°F (180°C). Line a 9- × 13-inch (3.5 L) baking pan with parchment paper.

2. Arrange the polenta in a single layer in the pan, slightly overlapping the rounds if needed. Drizzle with 1 Tbsp (15 mL) of the olive oil and sprinkle with the parmesan cheese. Bake for 20 minutes, until hot and light golden.

3. While the polenta is cooking, heat the remaining 2 Tbsp (30 mL) of olive oil in a very large, wide skillet over medium to medium-high heat. Add the mushrooms and cook until they release their moisture and become tender, 5 to 7 minutes.

4. Add the garlic, wine, and tarragon and simmer, watching closely, until the wine is reduced to 2 Tbsp (30 mL), 2 to 3 minutes.

5. Stir in the cream and chicken, and allow to come to a simmer. Cook until the cream has lightly thickened and the chicken is hot, 3 to 4 minutes. Season with salt and pepper.

6. Place 3 rounds of polenta in each shallow bowl. Top with the chicken/mushroom mixture, some blue cheese (or goat cheese), and parsley. Serve immediately.

Note: Look for tubes of ready-to-use polenta in Italian food stores and in the deli section of some supermarkets. Don't worry if the package you buy is not exactly the same size as the one called for in this recipe.

Panko-crusted Quinoa, Chickpea, and Chicken Cakes

These savory cakes are nutritious and delicious. Together, the quinoa and chickpeas provide plenty of fiber, iron, calcium, vitamin B6, riboflavin, and potassium. Chicken works well with both of these ingredients, especially when flavored with bold-tasting curry paste, fresh herbs, and lime juice.

Prep time: about 25 minutes, plus chilling time • Cooking time: 21 minutes • Makes: 4 servings (2 cakes each)

½ cup (125 mL) quinoa

1 cup (250 mL) water

1 can (19 oz/540 mL) chickpeas, drained, rinsed, and drained well again

1 Tbsp (15 mL) mild Indian-style curry paste

¾ cup (175 mL) finely diced rotisserie chicken meat

3 Tbsp (45 mL) chopped fresh cilantro or mint

2 green onions, thinly sliced

¼ cup (60 mL) coarsely grated carrots

1 large egg

1 Tbsp (15 mL) fresh lime juice

2 tsp (10 mL) honey

Salt to taste

¾ cup (175 mL) panko

3 Tbsp (45 mL) vegetable oil

⅓ cup (80 mL) mango chutney, or to taste

⅓ cup (80 mL) plain thick yogurt, or to taste

1. Place the quinoa and water in a small pot and bring to a boil over high heat. Cover the pot and reduce the heat to medium-low. Cook the quinoa, undisturbed, for 15 minutes, or until just tender and the water has evaporated. Allow to cool to room temperature.

2. In a medium to large bowl, use a potato masher to mash the chickpeas to a paste. Add the cooked quinoa, curry paste, chicken, cilantro (or mint), green onions, carrots, egg, lime juice, honey, and salt. Mix well to combine.

3. Line a baking sheet with parchment paper. Spread the panko on a very wide plate.

4. With damp hands, scoop ¼ to ⅓ cup (60 to 80 mL) of the quinoa mixture into a ball, then form it into a patty about ¾ inch (2 cm) thick. Repeat until you have 8 cakes.

5. Dredge each cake in panko, gently pressing on the crumbs to help them adhere, then set on the prepared baking sheet. Cover and refrigerate the cakes for 30 minutes to firm up. (They can be made to this point and refrigerated for several hours before cooking.)

6. When ready to serve, divide the vegetable oil between two large nonstick skillets and heat over medium to medium-high heat. When the oil is hot, add the cakes (4 per pan) and cook for 3 minutes per side, or until nicely colored and hot throughout.

7. Serve 2 cakes per person with a dollop of the chutney and yogurt alongside.

Rotisserie Chicken with Quick Summer Ratatouille

When local eggplants, zucchini, and bell peppers are at their finest, make this quick-cooking version of the traditional ratatouille, which better preserves the vegetables' individual colors and flavors. Serve the chicken and ratatouille with some miniature boiled potatoes tossed with butter and parsley, to create an inviting meal.

Prep time: 25 minutes • Cooking time: about 20 minutes • Makes: 4 servings

2 Tbsp (30 mL) olive oil

½ small eggplant, diced

1 small onion, diced

1 medium green bell pepper, diced

1 medium zucchini, diced

6 to 8 white or brown mushrooms, each
    quartered

2 garlic cloves, chopped

Pinch of dried, crushed chili flakes

1 can (14 oz/398 mL) diced tomatoes

2 Tbsp (30 mL) tomato paste

1 cup (250 mL) tomato sauce

½ cup (125 mL) chicken stock (page 59)

¼ cup (60 mL) chopped fresh basil

Salt and freshly ground black pepper
    to taste

¼ cup (60 mL) freshly grated parmesan
    cheese (optional)

1 rotisserie chicken, hot, cut into portions
    (page 16)

1. Heat olive oil in a wide pot or a skillet over medium to medium-high heat. Add the eggplant, onions, bell peppers, zucchini, mushrooms, garlic, and chili flakes, and cook until the mushrooms release their juices and become tender, 7 or 8 minutes.

2. Add the tomatoes, tomato paste, tomato sauce, and stock and bring to a simmer. Cook for 10 minutes, until the vegetables are quite tender, then stir in the basil. Season with salt and pepper and fold in the parmesan.

3. To serve, divide the ratatouille among 4 wide, shallow bowls. Arrange the chicken on top and serve.

Chicken and Vegetable Strata

This perfect brunch or lunch dish is basically a bread pudding—albeit a savory one—richly stocked with bits of chicken and loads of vegetables, herbs, and cheese. Cheddar works well, but you could also experiment with Gouda or asiago cheese or a combination.

Prep time: 30 minutes • Cooking time: 50 to 60 minutes • Makes: 8 servings

---

2 Tbsp (30 mL) olive oil, divided

½ lb (250 g) white or brown mushrooms, thinly sliced

1 medium zucchini, diced

1 small red bell pepper, diced

1 garlic clove, minced

Vegetable oil spray

1 brick (8 oz/250 g) cream cheese, room temperature

1 cup (250 mL) light cream

12 large eggs

Salt and white pepper to taste

1 tsp (5 mL) herbes de Provence (page 190)

1½ cups (375 mL) diced rotisserie chicken meat

½ day-old loaf French bread, cut in 1-inch (2.5 cm) cubes

3 green onions, thinly sliced

1½ cups (375 mL) grated aged cheddar cheese

1. Set 2 large skillets over medium to medium-high heat. Heat 1 Tbsp (15 mL) of the olive oil in each pan.

2. Place ½ the mushrooms, zucchini, bell peppers, and garlic in each skillet and sauté until the mushrooms release their juices and become tender, 7 to 8 minutes. Remove from the heat and allow the mixture to cool to room temperature.

3. Preheat the oven to 350°F (180°C). Grease a 9- × 13-inch (3.5 L) baking dish with vegetable oil spray.

4. In a large bowl, beat the cream cheese and cream until well combined (don't worry if it's not exactly smooth). Whisk in the eggs, salt and pepper, and herbes de Provence. Stir in the cooked vegetable mixture, chicken, bread, green onions, and ½ the cheese.

5. Spoon the bread mixture into the baking dish. Sprinkle with the remaining cheese and bake, uncovered, for 45 to 50 minutes, until golden and puffed in the center. Allow the strata to stand for 5 to 10 minutes before cutting and serving.

Rotisserie Chicken with Green Onion Mashed Potatoes and Mustard Sauce

This is a rich and fancy way to serve rotisserie chicken, and the recipe is not difficult to prepare. A green vegetable makes a perfect complement to the meal.

Prep time: 25 minutes • Cooking time: about 25 minutes • Makes: 4 servings

2 lb (1 kg) russet or Yukon Gold (yellow-fleshed) potatoes, peeled and quartered

¼ cup (60 mL) white wine or chicken stock (page 59)

Pinch of dried tarragon or thyme

1 small garlic clove, minced

1 cup (250 mL) whipping cream

¼ cup (60 mL) whole-grain Dijon mustard

½ cup (125 mL) buttermilk

2 Tbsp (30 mL) butter, room temperature

Salt and white pepper to taste

3 green onions, thinly sliced

1 rotisserie chicken, hot, cut into portions (page 16)

1. Place the potatoes in a pot and cover with a generous amount of cold water. Bring to a boil over high heat, then reduce the heat until the water is simmering (small bubbles should just be breaking on the surface). Simmer the potatoes until very tender, 18 to 20 minutes.

2. While the potatoes are cooking, combine the wine (or stock), tarragon (or thyme), and garlic in a small pot, bring to a boil over high heat, and reduce by half, about 2 minutes. Pour in the cream, bring to a simmer, and reduce until the sauce lightly thickens, 3 to 4 minutes. Stir in the mustard. Cover and keep warm over low heat.

3. Drain the potatoes well and, using a potato masher, mash thoroughly. Add the buttermilk and butter and beat until well combined. Season with salt and pepper, then stir in the green onions.

4. To serve, mound a scoop of the potatoes in the center of each dinner plate. Arrange the chicken on and around the potatoes, then drizzle with the mustard sauce. Enjoy.

Chicken and Black Bean Chili

Serve this hearty chili with a bowl of tortilla chips or Skillet Cornbread (page 188) to scoop up the sauce. Garnish the chili with grated Monterey Jack or cheddar cheese, chopped cilantro, and a dollop of sour cream or yogurt. This chili freezes beautifully. Allow it to cool to room temperature, pack it into airtight containers, label and date, and freeze for up to 3 months.

Prep time: 25 minutes • Cooking time: about 55 minutes • Makes: 8 to 10 servings

2 Tbsp (30 mL) vegetable oil

1 medium onion, diced

1 green bell pepper, diced

1 large celery stalk, diced

2 garlic cloves, chopped

1 can (28 oz/796 mL) crushed tomatoes

1 can (28 oz/796 mL) diced tomatoes

2 cans (each 19 oz/540 mL) black beans, drained, rinsed in cold water, and drained again

1½ cups (375 mL) beer or chicken stock (page 59)

2 cups (500 mL) diced rotisserie chicken meat

1 Tbsp (15 mL) chili powder

2 tsp (10 mL) ground cumin

1 tsp (5 mL) dried oregano

2 tsp (10 mL) hot pepper sauce, or to taste (page 88)

1 cup (250 mL) fresh or frozen corn kernels

Salt and freshly ground black pepper to taste

1. Heat the vegetable oil in a large pot or a Dutch oven over medium heat. Add the onions, bell peppers, celery, and garlic and cook for 5 to 6 minutes, until the vegetables are softened.

2. Mix in the remaining ingredients and bring to a gentle simmer. Partially cover and simmer for about 45 minutes, until the chili is richly flavored, thickened, and bubbly. Season with salt and pepper, if needed.

Teriyaki Chicken Stir-fry with Orange and Ginger

Teriyaki is a Japanese way of flavoring and glazing seafood or meat with a sweet and salty soy-based sauce. In this version, rather than grilling or broiling, as per usual, stir-frying imparts the teriyaki flavor. Make the stir-fry spicy by adding Asian-style hot chili sauce to taste when you pour in the teriyaki sauce mixture.

Prep time: 15 minutes • Cooking time: 10 minutes • Makes: 4 servings

---

⅔ cup (160 mL) teriyaki sauce (see Note)

½ cup (125 mL) orange or pineapple juice

1 Tbsp (15 mL) cornstarch

2 Tbsp (30 mL) water

2 Tbsp (30 mL) vegetable oil

24 small broccoli florets

½ cup (125 mL) diced red bell peppers

1 medium garlic clove, minced

1 tsp (5 mL) freshly grated ginger

½ a rotisserie chicken, meat removed and pulled into shreds

2 green onions, thinly sliced

1. In a small bowl, whisk together the teriyaki sauce, orange (or pineapple) juice, cornstarch, and water and set aside.

2. Heat the vegetable oil in a large nonstick skillet or wok over medium-high heat. When the oil is very hot, add the broccoli, bell peppers, garlic, and ginger and stir-fry for 2 minutes. Stir in the chicken and cook for 1 minute more.

3. Pour in the teriyaki sauce mixture and bring to a simmer. Cook, lightly tossing the vegetables and simmering them, for 2 minutes more, or until the chicken is hot and sauce forms around it. Sprinkle with green onions and serve.

Note: Use a thinner-style teriyaki sauce, such as Kikkoman brand, in this recipe. Thicker versions will become gluey when simmered and reduced.

HOW TO STIR-FRY

Have all the ingredients chopped ahead of time. Stir-frying means cooking food quickly over high heat, so ensure everything is ready to go before heating the pan.

Be sure the pan and the cooking oil are hot. Heat is the key to fried, seared, and nicely colored food. If the heat is too low, the ingredients will steam and become limp or oily by the time the pan comes up to temperature.

Keep the food moving. Stirring constantly prevents the ingredients from sticking to the wok and ensures everything gets cooked—and gets cooked evenly.

Quick Chicken Curry with Apples and Raisins

This dish is quick to make because the chicken is already cooked before being added to the sauce. The fruit, curry powder, and coconut milk provide a lovely flavor and create a sauce with an almost creamy texture. If you like spicy, use a medium or hot curry powder.

Prep time: 20 minutes • Cooking time: about 15 minutes • Makes: 3 to 4 servings

1 Tbsp (15 mL) vegetable oil

½ cup (125 mL) diced onions

½ cup (125 mL) diced celery rib

1 tsp (5 mL) chopped fresh ginger

2 tsp (10 mL) mild curry powder

1 can (14 oz/398 mL) coconut milk

⅓ cup (80 mL) chicken stock

1 Tbsp (15 mL) lime juice

1 Tbsp (15 mL) brown sugar

1½ to 2 cups (375 to 500 mL) diced rotisserie chicken meat

1 medium red apple, unpeeled but cored and cut into small cubes

¼ cup (60 mL) raisins

2 Tbsp (30 mL) chopped fresh cilantro

Salt to taste

1. Heat the vegetable oil in a 10-inch (25 cm) wide, heavy-bottomed pot over medium-high. Add the onions, celery, and ginger and cook for 2 minutes. Stir in the curry powder and cook for 1 minute more.

2. Pour in the coconut milk, stock, lime juice, and sugar, and then add the chicken, apples, and raisins. Bring to a gentle simmer, reducing the heat if necessary to maintain a gentle simmer. Cook for 10 minutes, or until flavorful.

3. Stir in the cilantro, season with a little salt, and serve.

Chicken Tikka Masala

Great Britain's fondness for Indian food has simmered to such heights that chicken tikka masala has become a national dish. There are several ways to make it, and this fairly spicy version uses the meat from a rotisserie chicken. Make a meal of this chicken dish by serving it with steamed basmati rice; wedges of naan, pita bread, or Cumin Seed Chapattis (page 185); and steamed broccoli drizzled with melted butter and freshly squeezed lime juice.

Prep time: 30 minutes • Cooking time: 28 minutes • Makes: 4 servings

2 tsp (10 mL) garam masala (see Note)

1 tsp (5 mL) paprika

½ tsp (2 mL) ground cardamom

½ tsp (2 mL) ground cumin

½ tsp (2 mL) ground coriander seeds

¼ tsp (1 mL) ground turmeric

½ tsp (2 mL) cayenne pepper, or to taste

¼ tsp (1 mL) ground cinnamon

2 Tbsp (30 mL) vegetable oil

1 medium onion, finely chopped

1 Tbsp (15 mL) tomato paste

1 Tbsp (15 mL) finely grated fresh ginger

1 large garlic clove, minced

1 can (14 oz/398 mL) diced tomatoes

1¼ cups (310 mL) chicken stock
   (page 59)

1 rotisserie chicken, meat removed and
   cut in ¾-inch (2 cm) cubes

3 Tbsp (45 mL) plain yogurt or whipping
   cream

Salt to taste

Sprigs of fresh cilantro, for garnish
   (optional)

1. In a small bowl, combine the garam masala, paprika, cardamom, cumin, coriander seed, turmeric, cayenne pepper, and cinnamon. Set this spice mixture aside.

2. Heat the vegetable oil in a large, deep skillet over medium to medium-high heat. Add the onions and cook until softened and light golden, 5 to 7 minutes.

3. Stir in the spice mixture, tomato paste, ginger, and garlic and cook, stirring, for 2 minutes more. Add the diced tomatoes and stock, bring to a gentle simmer, and cook for 10 minutes.

4. Add the chicken and continue to simmer until the chicken is nicely flavored and the sauce has thickened, 6 to 8 minutes.

5. Stir in the yogurt (or cream) and heat through for 1 minute. Adjust seasoning, if needed, and serve. Garnish with sprigs of cilantro, if desired.

Note: Garam masala is an Indian-style spice blend available in the spice aisle of many supermarkets and Asian food stores. The number and quantity of the spices in garam masala can vary, but many contain cloves, cinnamon, cumin, and cardamom.

Cajun-spiced Char-grilled Corn (page 166)

MAKING YOUR ROTISSERIE CHICKEN A MEAL

Side Dishes for Your Storebought or Homecooked Chicken

SIDE
SALADS

Zucchini Pickles pictured with
Ale-marinated Mushroom Salad (page 155)

Fresh Zucchini Pickles

More a condiment than a salad, these no-canning-required, easy-to-make pickles taste great served alongside rotisserie chicken. They do require an overnight soak in the refrigerator to infuse them with a sweet and tangy flavor, so start these pickles the day before you plan to serve them. You'll need one 4-cup (1 L) glass jar in which to make them.

Prep time: 10 minutes, plus marinating time • Cooking time: a few minutes • Makes: about 8 servings

1 cup (250 mL) cider vinegar

⅓ cup (80 mL) granulated sugar

½ tsp (2 mL) salt

4 tsp (20 mL) whole-grain Dijon mustard

1 Tbsp (15 mL) chopped fresh dill

Coarsely ground black pepper to taste

4 cups (1 L) sliced zucchini (see Note)

1. Heat the vinegar, sugar, and salt in a small pot over medium heat until the sugar and salt have just dissolved. Allow to cool to room temperature, then stir in the mustard, dill, and pepper.

2. Layer the zucchini slices into the jar. (The jar used when testing the recipe was 4½ inches/11.5 cm wide.)

3. Pour the vinegar mixture over the zucchini, firmly pushing down on the slices to ensure they are at least partially submerged. The top slices will sink as they marinate.

4. Tightly seal the jar and refrigerate overnight (at least 12 hours). Enjoy pickles now. Any leftovers will keep refrigerated for up to 2 weeks.

Note: Small zucchini are best for this recipe. The ones I used were about 7 inches (17.5 cm) long and 1½ inches (3.75 cm) wide, and I cut them in slices ¼ inch (6 mm) thick. I used three zucchini to get the 4 cups (1 L) needed for this recipe.

Salad Greens with Peaches, Brie, and Cashews

Rich with fruit, cheese, and nuts, this salad looks pretty on a plate with a quarter piece of rotisserie chicken served alongside. Play around with the greens, substituting spinach or chopped leaf lettuce, or try pecan halves in place of the cashews. This salad combination should pair well with Maple-Mustard Chicken with Coriander and Pepper (page 28).

Prep time: 10 minutes • Cooking time: none • Makes: 4 servings

1½ Tbsp (22.5 mL) cider vinegar

1 tsp (5 mL) Dijon mustard

2 tsp (10 mL) honey

1 Tbsp (15 mL) chopped fresh mint

4½ Tbsp (67.5 mL) olive oil

Salt and freshly ground black pepper
   to taste

8 cups (2 L) mixed baby salad greens

2 medium ripe peaches, cut in thin wedges

5 oz (150 g) brie cheese, cut in small cubes

½ cup (125 mL) unsalted roasted cashews

1. Place the vinegar, mustard, honey, mint, and olive oil in a salad bowl and whisk to combine. Season the dressing with salt and pepper.
2. Add the salad greens and toss to coat them with the dressing. Divide the greens among 4 plates. Arrange the peach wedges, cheese, and cashews on the salad greens and serve.

Spinach and Vegetable Salad
with Lemon-Tarragon Yogurt Dressing

Tender, earthy-tasting baby spinach and colorful vegetables tossed with a light yogurt-based salad dressing make a refreshing contrast to rich and juicy rotisserie chicken. Serve this salad with storebought rotisserie chicken, or one you made yourself, such as Piri Piri Chicken (page 27).

Prep time: 15 minutes • Cooking time: none • Makes: 4 to 6 servings

½ cup (125 mL) no-fat, plain yogurt

2 Tbsp (30 mL) fresh lemon juice

1 Tbsp (15 mL) honey, or to taste

1 Tbsp (15 mL) olive oil

2 tsp (10 mL) chopped fresh tarragon or
   ½ tsp (2 mL) dried

Salt and white pepper to taste

8 cups (2 L) baby spinach

½ small red onion, thinly sliced

1 small carrot, halved lengthwise and
   thinly sliced on the bias

½ medium yellow bell pepper, cut in
   small cubes

12 cherry tomatoes, halved

⅓ English cucumber, halved and sliced

1. Place the yogurt, lemon juice, honey, olive oil, and tarragon in a salad bowl and whisk to combine. Season the dressing with salt and white pepper.
2. Add the spinach, onions, carrots, bell peppers, cherry tomatoes, and cucumber. Toss to coat with the dressing and combine. Serve immediately.

Leaf Lettuce Salad with Ranch Dressing, Bacon Bits, and Tomatoes

You could call this a BLT (bacon, lettuce, and tomato) sandwich minus the bread but drizzled with an irresistible and creamy homemade ranch dressing. Serve it alongside storebought rotisserie chicken, or try it with Traditional Barbecued Rotisserie Chicken (page 20) or Maple-Mustard Chicken with Coriander and Pepper (page 28).

Prep time: 15 minutes • Cooking time: about 6 minutes (for the bacon) • Makes: 4 servings

---

⅓ cup (80 mL) mayonnaise

⅓ cup (80 mL) sour cream

2 Tbsp (30 mL) lemon juice

½ tsp (2 mL) granulated sugar

2 Tbsp (30 mL) snipped fresh chives or very thinly sliced green onions

Salt and white pepper to taste

1 small to medium head leaf lettuce, trimmed, washed, dried, and chopped

2 medium ripe tomatoes, cut in thin wedges

6 slices bacon, cut in half lengthwise, diced, cooked crisply, and drained well

1. To make the dressing, in a small bowl, combine the mayonnaise, sour cream, lemon juice, sugar, and chives (or green onions). Season with salt and pepper. Set aside.

2. Divide the lettuce among 4 plates. Top the salad with the tomato wedges and bacon. Serve the dressing in a separate bowl and allow guests to spoon it over their own salads.

Sweet and Sour Coleslaw with Cranberries and Apricots

Made with vibrantly colored cranberries, apricots, and grated carrots and dressed with a vinaigrette, this coleslaw is a departure from the more traditional versions dressed with mayonnaise. Try it with Traditional Barbecued Rotisserie Chicken (page 20) or Moroccan-spiced Chicken (page 24). It will also taste great alongside a storebought rotisserie chicken. Halve the recipe if you're not feeding a crowd.

Prep time: 15 minutes • Cooking time: none • Makes: 8 to 10 servings

3 Tbsp (45 mL) raspberry or cider vinegar

2 Tbsp (30 mL) vegetable oil

1 Tbsp (15 mL) honey

2 tsp (10 mL) Dijon mustard

Salt and freshly ground black pepper
   to taste

4 cups (1 L) finely shredded green cabbage
   (about ½ small head)

⅔ cup (160 mL) dried cranberries

12 dried apricots, thinly sliced lengthwise

1 cup (250 mL) coarsely grated carrots

3 green onions, thinly sliced

1. In a large bowl, combine the vinegar, vegetable oil, honey, mustard, and salt and pepper until well mixed.
2. Add the cabbage, cranberries, apricots, carrots, and green onions. Toss well to coat with the dressing and combine, and serve.

ABOUT GREEN CABBAGE

The word "cabbage" is derived from the French *caboche*, which means "head" and is a clear reference to its shape. The most common head cabbage is green cabbage; other types include red and savoy. They are often interchangeable, though cooked red cabbage will turn any dish a purplish color.

When purchasing, choose well-shaped heads that feel heavy for their size and have fresh, crisp-looking leaves. Store a whole head of cabbage in a plastic bag in your refrigerator crisper. If it's in good condition, it will keep a week or more. Once cut, cabbage deteriorates fairly quickly and should be used within a few days. Cabbage is an excellent source of minerals and vitamins A, C, and B—all good reasons to eat it.

Orange, Avocado, and Red Onion Salad

This light salad is quick to assemble, but you could make the dressing in advance to save time. Try serving it while dining al fresco with Traditional Barbecued Rotisserie Chicken (page 20), Spanish-style Chicken (page 23), or Moroccan-spiced Chicken (page 24). To switch things up, when in season, try slices of blood orange in this salad.

Prep time: 25 minutes • Cooking time: none • Makes: 6 servings

2 Tbsp (30 mL) fresh orange juice

1 Tbsp (15 mL) cider vinegar

3 Tbsp (45 mL) olive oil

2 tsp (10 mL) honey

2 tsp (10 mL) Dijon mustard

Salt and freshly ground black pepper
   to taste

1 large ripe avocado, quartered lengthwise, peeled, and sliced widthwise

2 tsp (10 mL) fresh lemon juice

12 butter or leaf lettuce leaves

5 medium oranges, peel and pith removed,
   flesh cut in slices ¼ inch (6 mm) thick

½ medium red onion, halved and very
   thinly sliced

2 Tbsp (30 mL) chopped fresh cilantro
   or mint

1. To make the dressing, in a small bowl, combine the orange juice, vinegar, olive oil, honey, mustard, and salt and pepper.

2. Place the avocado and lemon juice in a medium bowl and toss to combine.

3. Line a platter with the lettuce leaves and arrange the orange slices over them. Top with the onions and avocado.

4. Drizzle the salad with the dressing, sprinkle with cilantro (or mint), and serve.

Creamy and Comforting Cucumber Salad

Cool and creamy, this is a cucumber salad my mom used to make routinely when I was a child, and it conjures happy memories of home. Serve it as an accompaniment for Traditional Barbecued Rotisserie Chicken (page 20) or a storebought chicken.

Prep time: 15 minutes, plus salting time • Cooking time: none • Makes: 8 servings

2 medium field cucumbers, peeled and halved lengthwise

½ tsp (2 mL) salt

3 Tbsp (45 mL) mayonnaise

3 Tbsp (45 mL) sour cream

1 tsp (5 mL) white vinegar

1 tsp (5 mL) Dijon mustard

1 tsp (5 mL) chopped fresh dill or tarragon or chives

½ tsp (2 mL) granulated sugar

Pinch of ground white pepper

1. Using a small spoon, scrape out and discard the seeds from the cucumbers.
2. Slice the cucumbers, widthwise, into slices ¼ inch (6 mm) thick, and place in a bowl. Toss in the salt, cover, and allow the cucumbers to stand for 1 hour.
3. Drain excess water from the cucumbers.
4. In a small bowl, combine the remaining ingredients. Spoon over the cucumbers and toss to combine. Serve immediately.

Ale-marinated Mushroom Salad

I live in Victoria, B.C., which is home to an amazing array of microbreweries. When sampling beers, I always wonder how they could enhance a dish and that, in turn, leads me to try using them in recipes. Here, the amber ale adds a pleasing bitter edge to the marinade for this mushroom salad. Start the dish a day ahead of time, then pack it up with some cold pieces of rotisserie chicken meat to enjoy at a picnic.

Prep time: 10 minutes, plus marinating time • Cooking time: about 10 minutes • Makes: about 2 cups

1 lb (500 g) small fresh white or brown mushrooms (see Note)

¾ cup (175 mL) amber ale

1 large garlic clove, minced

3 Tbsp (45 mL) lemon juice

¼ cup (60 mL) extra-virgin olive oil

2 Tbsp (30 mL) Dijon mustard

2 tsp (10 mL) Worcestershire sauce

½ tsp (2 mL) Tabasco sauce

Pinch of dried thyme

1 Tbsp (15 mL) chopped fresh parsley

1. Place the mushrooms, ale, and garlic in a large skillet over medium heat. Simmer until the mushrooms are softened, about 5 minutes. Using a slotted spoon, transfer the cooked mushrooms to a small bowl.

2. Reduce the liquid left in the skillet to about 2 Tbsp (30 mL), then pour it over the mushrooms.

3. In a second small bowl, combine the remaining ingredients. Pour this mixture over the mushrooms and toss to combine. Allow the mushrooms to cool to room temperature.

4. Cover, refrigerate, and marinate mushrooms for at least 4 hours before serving.

Note: To clean the mushrooms before cooking, simply wipe off any debris with a paper towel. If you feel you must wash them, set them in a bowl of cold water and very quickly and gently swirl to clean. Get them out of the bowl as soon as possible and dry them on paper towels. Doing so will ensure they don't absorb water.

Southern-spiced Yam and Black Bean Salad

When I create recipes, I often begin by listing the key ingredients I want to use. I then consider what would marry well with them. For this salad, I started with sweet yams and earthy black beans, which I associate with Southern locales, then matched them with cilantro, lime, corn, and chilies. This salad works well with Piri Piri Chicken (page 27) and Jerk Chicken (page 25). Note that it yields a generous amount, but any leftover salad will taste great the next day, perhaps used in a wrap with leftover chicken.

Prep time: 25 minutes • Cooking time: about 5 minutes • Makes: 10 to 12 servings

2 lb (1 kg) yams, peeled and cut in 1/2-inch (1.25 cm) cubes (about 3 medium)

¼ cup (60 mL) lime juice

¼ cup (60 mL) orange juice

½ cup (125 mL) olive oil

2 tsp (10 mL) honey

1 large garlic clove, minced

1 tsp (5 mL) ground cumin

1 tsp (5 mL) chili powder

2 tsp (10 mL) hot pepper sauce, such as Tabasco, or to taste

1 can (19 oz/540 mL) black beans, drained, rinsed, and drained again

½ small red onion, finely diced

1 medium green bell pepper, finely diced

1 cup (250 mL) fresh or frozen corn kernels, thawed

⅓ cup (80 mL) chopped fresh cilantro or mint or sliced green onions

Salt and freshly ground black pepper to taste

1. Place the yams in a pot, cover them with cold water, and bring to a simmer over medium heat. Cook until just tender but still holding their shape, about 5 minutes. (Do not overcook or they'll break apart in the salad.) Drain well, cool in cold water, and drain again.

2. To make the dressing, combine the lime and orange juices, olive oil, honey, garlic, cumin, chili powder, and hot pepper sauce in a salad bowl. Add the yams and the remaining ingredients and toss to combine. Cover and refrigerate until ready to serve. Toss again gently before serving.

Note: There's a fairly generous amount of juice and oil in this salad because the yams and beans act like sponges, soaking up the flavor.

Miniature Potato Salad with Grainy Dijon and Chives

Miniature new potatoes are 1 to 2 inches (2.5 to 5 cm) in diameter and come in white, red, yellow-fleshed, and purple varieties. Use a mix of colors in this classic salad, which is great at a picnic served with Traditional Barbecued Rotisserie Chicken (page 20) or a storebought rotisserie chicken.

Prep time: 10 minutes • Cooking time: 10 to 15 minutes • Makes: 8 servings

---

2 lb (1 kg) miniature new potatoes

⅔ cup (160 mL) mayonnaise

2 Tbsp (30 mL) white wine vinegar

1 celery stalk, finely chopped

2 Tbsp (30 mL) whole-grain Dijon mustard

2 Tbsp (30 mL) snipped fresh chives or thinly sliced green onions

Salt and freshly ground black pepper to taste

2 large hard-boiled eggs, cooled and chopped

1. Wash the potatoes well, but do not peel them. Cut the potatoes into quarters, place them in a pot, and cover with cold water. Bring to a boil over high heat, then cook until just tender, 7 to 8 minutes. Drain well, transfer to a bowl, and allow to cool to room temperature.

2. Mix in the remaining ingredients, reserving a few of the snipped chives (or green onions) as a garnish. Cover and refrigerate the salad until needed. When ready to serve, sprinkle it with the remaining chives (or green onions).

ABOUT CHIVES

Chives come from the same Allium family as onions, and because they are easy to grow, they are a staple in many backyard or patio herb gardens. Chives are usually harvested before they flower, which preserves their delicate flavor. Pick them from your garden or purchase them when they are bright green and evenly colored. If they're very fresh, cut chives will keep refrigerated for several days in a plastic bag or the plastic container they came in. Use kitchen scissors to snip them into salads and other dishes.

Curried Rice and Lentil Salad

This sweet, nicely spiced Indian-style rice salad is enhanced with a nutritious mix of lentils, vegetables, and dried fruit. It yields a generous 10 servings, but any leftovers will taste just fine the next day, or the day after that. Try pairing this salad with Tandoori Chicken (page 30) or Red Thai Curry Chicken (page 32).

Prep time: 25 minutes • Cooking time: about 20 minutes • Makes: 10 servings

1½ cups (375 mL) basmati or long-grain white rice

2 tsp (10 mL) mild or medium curry powder

2¼ cups (560 mL) chicken (page 59) or vegetable stock

1 can (19 oz/540 mL) lentils, drained, rinsed, and drained well again

1 cup (250 mL) whole almonds, skins on

½ cup (125 mL) grated carrots

½ cup (125 mL) diced celery

½ cup (125 mL) dried cranberries or raisins

¼ cup (60 mL) chopped fresh mint

3 green onions, thinly sliced

2 Tbsp (30 mL) vegetable oil

½ cup (125 mL) orange juice

2 Tbsp (30 mL) lime juice

1 Tbsp (15 mL) honey

Salt and freshly ground black pepper to taste

1. Place the rice, curry powder, and stock in a medium pot and bring to a boil over high heat. Reduce the heat to its lowest setting, cover, and cook until the rice is tender, 15 to 18 minutes. Fluff the rice with a fork, transfer to a large bowl, and allow to cool to room temperature.

2. Add the remaining ingredients and toss to combine. Cover and refrigerate the salad until ready to serve. It can be made many hours ahead. Toss again gently before serving.

Quinoa and Chickpea Tabbouleh

This twist on the classic Middle Eastern salad tosses in quinoa instead of the usual bulgur wheat. Chickpeas and cherry tomatoes add even more nutrition, texture, and color. The salad will nicely complement succulent pieces of Moroccan-spiced Chicken (page 24).

Prep time: 25 minutes • Cooking time: 15 minutes • Makes: 8 servings

1¼ cups (310 mL) quinoa

2 cups (500 mL) water

1 can (19 oz/540 mL) chickpeas, drained, rinsed, and drained again

⅓ cup (80 mL) olive oil

2 tsp (10 mL) finely grated lemon zest

3 Tbsp (45 mL) fresh lemon juice

1 cup (250 mL) chopped fresh parsley

¼ cup (60 mL) finely chopped fresh mint

18 cherry tomatoes, halved

½ medium English cucumber, cut in small cubes

1½ tsp (7 mL) ground cumin

1 tsp (5 mL) paprika

Pinch of cayenne pepper

Salt and freshly ground black pepper to taste

1. Place the quinoa and water in a medium pot and bring to a boil over high heat. Cover the pot and reduce the heat to medium-low. Cook the quinoa, undisturbed, for 15 minutes, or until just tender and the water has evaporated.

2. Spoon the cooked quinoa into a large salad bowl and allow to cool to room temperature. Add the remaining ingredients and toss to combine.

3. Cover and refrigerate the salad until needed. It can be made several hours ahead. Toss again gently before serving.

HOT SIDE DISHES

Green Beans with Tahini Sauce

Tahini is a paste made from sesame seeds, which are rich in nutrients, and is often used in Middle Eastern and Mediterranean-style cooking. Look for it in the ethnic food aisle of most supermarkets. In this recipe, tahini is blended with citrus juices, mint, and cumin to flavor the green beans. Serve this side dish with Moroccan-spiced Chicken (page 24) or Maple-Mustard Chicken with Coriander and Pepper (page 28).

Prep time: 10 minutes • Cooking time: 2 to 3 minutes • Makes: 4 to 6 servings

¼ cup (60 mL) tahini

¼ cup (60 mL) orange juice

1 Tbsp (15 mL) lemon juice

2 Tbsp (30 mL) chopped fresh mint

1 small garlic clove, minced

⅛ tsp (0.5 mL) ground cumin

Salt and freshly ground black pepper
  to taste

1¼ lb (625 g) fresh green beans, trimmed

1 tsp (5 mL) finely grated lemon zest,
  for garnish

1. Bring a large pot of water to a boil over high heat.

2. While the water comes to temperature, make the dressing by combining the tahini, orange juice, lemon juice, mint, garlic, and cumin in a small bowl. Season with salt and pepper.

3. Add the green beans to the boiling water and cook until just tender, 2 to 3 minutes. Drain well.

4. Arrange the beans on a serving platter and drizzle with the tahini dressing. Sprinkle with lemon zest and serve.

Harvard Beets

This version of the classic New England–style beet dish is simmered in a sweet-and-sour sauce that glazes the vegetables and infuses them with flavor. Although it's not clear where the name came from, some people suggest the dramatic color of the beets resembles Harvard University's official crimson football jersey. Regardless of their origin, these beets would taste great alongside Sunday Dinner Rotisserie Chicken (page 33).

Prep time: 15 minutes • Cooking time: about 35 minutes • Makes: 6 servings

1 lb (500 g) medium beets (3 to 4)

⅓ cup (80 mL) granulated sugar

⅓ cup (80 mL) water

1 tsp (10 mL) cornstarch

3 Tbsp (45 mL) cider vinegar

1 Tbsp (15 mL) vegetable oil

Salt and freshly ground black pepper
    to taste

1. Place the beets in a pot, cover with cold water, and bring to a simmer over medium to medium-high heat. Cook for 25 to 30 minutes, or until tender. Drain well, cover the beets with cold water, and allow to cool.

2. Using your fingers or a sharp knife, peel the beets and discard the skins. Cut the beets into small cubes and place in a bowl.

3. Combine the sugar, water, cornstarch, vinegar, and vegetable oil in a skillet and simmer over medium-high heat until the sugar is dissolved, about 1 minute. Stir in the beets and allow to simmer for 5 minutes, stirring occasionally. Serve hot.

Cajun-spiced Char-grilled Corn

Cooked and served straight from the grill with a hint of spice or a squeeze of lemon or lime juice, corn is a popular street food in many parts of the world. This recipe allows you to serve it up in your own backyard in summer, when local corn is at its peak. For curry-spiced corn, replace the Cajun spice with an equal amount of curry powder.

Prep time: 10 minutes • Cooking time: 5 minutes • Makes: 6 servings

2 Tbsp (30 mL) melted butter

2 to 3 tsp (10 to 15 mL) Cajun spice

6 ears of fresh corn, shucked

Soft butter to taste

1 lime, cut in 6 wedges, for squeezing

1. Preheat a barbecue or indoor grill to medium or medium-high.
2. In a small bowl, combine the butter and Cajun spice until well mixed. Brush some of the mixture on each cob of corn.
3. Grill the corn, turning the cobs from time to time, until lightly charred and just tender, about 5 minutes.
4. Serve the corn on individual plates or on a platter with soft butter on the side, and garnish with wedges of lime.

Grilled Zucchini with Pine Nuts and Parmesan

One zucchini plant can yield at least ten zucchini, all ready for harvest around the same time. No wonder the avid gardeners in my neighborhood keep bringing me some! If you need a tasty way to use up your own zucchini, try grilling them to impart a smoky taste and then dressing them up Mediterranean-style with olive oil, balsamic vinegar, fresh basil, pine nuts, and parmesan cheese. This side dish would complement Spanish-style Chicken (page 23), Moroccan-spiced Chicken (page 24), or Piri Piri Chicken (page 27). For added richness, top the salad with ½ cup (125 mL) of coarsely crumbled feta cheese.

Prep time: 20 minutes • Cooking time: 2 to 4 minutes • Makes: 6 servings

1 medium green zucchini, cut diagonally in ½-inch (1.25 cm) thick slices

1 medium yellow zucchini, cut diagonally in ½-inch (1.25 cm) thick slices

4 Tbsp (60 mL) olive oil, divided

Salt and freshly ground black pepper to taste

2 Tbsp (30 mL) balsamic vinegar

8 fresh basil leaves, cut into large pieces

¼ cup (60 mL) pine nuts, lightly toasted (see Note)

⅓ cup (80 mL) thinly shaved parmesan cheese (see Note)

1. Preheat a barbecue or indoor grill to medium-high.

2. Place the zucchini slices in a bowl and toss with 2 Tbsp (30 mL) of the olive oil. Season with salt and pepper.

3. Grill the zucchini for 1 to 2 minutes per side, or until nicely colored and just tender. Transfer to a baking sheet and allow to cool to room temperature.

4. Arrange the zucchini on a large platter, drizzle with the remaining olive oil and the balsamic vinegar, then sprinkle with the basil, pine nuts, and parmesan. Serve.

Note: To toast pine nuts, preheat the oven to 300°F (150°C). Arrange the pine nuts in a single layer in a small baking pan and bake, shaking the dish from time to time, for 10 to 15 minutes, or until lightly toasted. To slice a piece of parmesan cheese into thin shavings, use a vegetable peeler.

Pesto-roasted Red Potatoes

This potato side dish can thank pesto for its aromatic qualities. The recipe makes more pesto than you'll need to flavor the potatoes, but you can freeze the unused portion in ice cube trays, then transfer the cubes to a resealable plastic bag. Keep pesto frozen, at the ready for the next time you need some, up to 3 months. If you don't wish to make your own pesto, simply use storebought pesto instead.

Prep time: 15 minutes • Cooking time: 43 to 48 minutes • Makes: 6 servings

Pesto

4 cups (1 L) loosely packed fresh basil
  leaves

3 medium garlic cloves, sliced

⅓ cup (80 mL) pine nuts, slivered
  almonds, or walnut pieces

½ cup (125 mL) freshly grated parmesan
  cheese

1 cup (250 mL) olive oil

Roasted potatoes

2 lb (1 kg) miniature red potatoes
  (page 158), washed well, dried,
  and halved

3 Tbsp (45 mL) pesto

1 Tbsp (15 mL) olive oil

1 Tbsp (15 mL) fresh lemon juice or
  balsamic vinegar

Salt and freshly ground black pepper
  to taste

Pesto

1. Place all the ingredients, except the olive oil, in a food processor and pulse until chopped.

2. Add the olive oil in a thin stream and process until well blended. If your pesto is too thick, add a bit more olive oil. Transfer to an airtight container or freeze in ice cube trays.

Roasted potatoes

1. Preheat the oven to 400°F (200°C). Line a baking sheet with parchment paper.

2. Place the potatoes in a large pot, cover with cold water, and bring to a boil over medium heat. Cook until the outer edges become just tender but the potatoes are still solidly holding their shape, about 8 minutes. Drain well, then place in a bowl.

3. Add the pesto, olive oil, and lemon juice (or balsamic vinegar) and toss to combine. Season with salt and pepper.

4. Arrange the potatoes in a single layer on the prepared baking sheet, then roast for 35 to 40 minutes, or until tender and nicely crusted with the pesto. Serve hot or at room temperature.

Garlic Mashed Potatoes with Kale

Kale is now very much in demand because its deep, slightly bitter, earthy flavor is appealing to a wider range of palates. Also, and perhaps more importantly, people have learned that kale is a good source of fiber, vitamins, and minerals (page 65). These garlic-infused spuds are mashed and mixed with kale, and they make a fine accompaniment for Traditional Barbecued Rotisserie Chicken (page 20) or Sunday Dinner Rotisserie Chicken (page 33).

Prep time: 15 minutes • Cooking time: 21 to 24 minutes • Makes: 4 servings

1½ lb (750 g) yellow-fleshed potatoes, peeled and quartered

4 large garlic cloves, thickly sliced

6 medium fresh kale leaves, washed well, tough lower stems trimmed (page 65)

¾ cup (175 mL) chicken stock (page 59)

2 Tbsp (30 mL) melted butter

Salt and white pepper to taste

1. Place the potatoes and garlic in a pot, cover with cold water, and bring to a simmer over medium to medium-high heat. Cook until very tender, 18 to 20 minutes.

2. While the potatoes are cooking, cut the kale leaves in half lengthwise, then widthwise into strips ¼ inch (6 mm) wide.

3. Bring the stock to a simmer over medium to medium-high heat in a deep, wide skillet. Add the kale and cook until just tender, 3 to 4 minutes. Remove from the heat and set aside the kale and cooking liquid.

4. Drain the potatoes well, ensuring the garlic stays in the pot. Using a potato masher, mash the potatoes and garlic thoroughly until as smooth as possible.

5. Stir in the butter and reserved kale and cooking liquid, and season with salt and pepper. Serve hot.

Chili-spiced Potato Wedges with Parmesan and Parsley

Roasted potatoes and chicken are a classic combination. Nestle these cheesy, chili-spiced wedges alongside Traditional Barbecued Rotisserie Chicken (page 20) or a storebought rotisserie chicken.

Prep time: 10 minutes • Cooking time: 40 minutes • Makes: 4 to 6 servings

3 large baking potatoes, unpeeled, washed well and patted dry

2 Tbsp (30 mL) olive oil

1 Tbsp (15 mL) chili powder

½ tsp (2 mL) ground cumin

1 tsp (5 mL) hot pepper sauce (page 88)

Salt to taste

⅓ cup (80 mL) freshly grated parmesan cheese, for garnish

2 Tbsp (30 mL) chopped fresh parsley, for garnish

1. Preheat the oven to 375°F (190°C). Line a large baking sheet with parchment paper.

2. Cut the potatoes in half lengthwise, then cut each half, lengthwise, into 6 wedges. Place the potato wedges in a bowl.

3. Add the olive oil, chili powder, cumin, pepper sauce, and salt and toss until the potatoes are well coated. Arrange the potatoes in a single layer on the prepared baking sheet and roast for 40 minutes, turning once halfway through cooking to ensure even browning.

4. Arrange the potatoes on a large serving platter, sprinkle with the parmesan and parsley, and serve.

Vegetable Chop Suey with Cashews

This vegetable-rich version of the classic Chinese-style dish served in North American restaurants is a great side dish, not surprisingly, with Chinese-style Barbecue Chicken (page 29). Legend suggests that chop suey is derived from *shap sui*, which means "odds and ends" or "mixed pieces" in Mandarin, and was first made in the 1800s by Chinese immigrants during California's gold rush. Like *shap sui*, the contemporary dish is often made from whatever ingredients the cook has on hand. Add a large bowl of steamed rice to complete the meal.

Prep time: 20 minutes • Cooking time: about 6 minutes • Makes: 4 to 6 servings

⅓ cup (80 mL) chicken stock (page 59)

1 tsp (5 mL) cornstarch

2 Tbsp (30 mL) soy sauce

1 tsp (5 mL) honey

1 tsp (5 mL) Asian-style hot chili sauce, or to taste (page 88)

2 Tbsp (30 mL) vegetable oil

1 medium garlic clove, minced

2 to 3 tsp (10 to 15 mL) finely chopped fresh ginger

1 medium onion, thinly sliced

1 medium carrot, halved lengthwise, thinly sliced diagonally

1 medium celery stalk, halved lengthwise, thinly sliced diagonally

½ medium red bell pepper, cubed

6 white or brown mushrooms, sliced

1½ cups (375 mL) bean sprouts

3 green onions, cut in 1-inch (2.5 cm) pieces

½ cup (125 mL) unsalted roasted cashews, coarsely chopped

1. In a small bowl, combine the stock, cornstarch, soy sauce, honey, and chili sauce until well mixed, then set aside.

2. Heat the vegetable oil in a large skillet or a wok over medium-high heat. Add the garlic, ginger, onions, carrots, celery, bell peppers, and mushrooms and stir-fry for 3 to 4 minutes, until the vegetables start to soften slightly.

3. Stir in the cornstarch mixture and bring to a simmer. Toss in the bean sprouts, green onions, and cashews and heat through for a few seconds. Serve immediately.

Red Lentil Dhal

In India, dhal refers to lentils and the spicy soups or side dishes made with them. This red lentil dhal is the latter. Try serving it with Tandoori Chicken (page 30).

Prep time: 10 minutes • Cooking time: about 35 minutes • Makes: 4 to 6 servings

2 Tbsp (30 mL) vegetable oil

1 small onion, finely chopped

1 large garlic clove, minced

1 Tbsp (15 mL) finely chopped fresh ginger

2 tsp (10 mL) mild curry powder

2 Tbsp (30 mL) tomato paste

1 cup (250 mL) dried red lentils, rinsed
   in cold water and drained well

3½ cups (875 mL) chicken stock (page 59)

¼ cup (60 mL) chopped fresh cilantro

Salt to taste

1. Heat the vegetable oil in a medium pot over medium heat. Add the onions, garlic, and ginger and cook until softened, about 5 minutes. Stir in the curry powder and tomato paste and cook for 1 minute more.

2. Mix in the lentils and stock and bring the mixture to a slow, gently bubbling simmer. Adjust the heat as needed. Allow to simmer for 30 minutes, or until the lentils are tender and the mixture has the consistency of stew.

3. Stir in the cilantro, season with salt, and serve.

ABOUT LENTILS

Lentils are the dried edible seeds of a legume and they come in many sizes and colors. They are all rich in protein, low in calories, fat, and cholesterol, and, among other good things, contain fiber, potassium, and iron.

The most common dried lentils sold in supermarkets are earthy-tasting green lentils and faster-cooking red lentils. Store them in an airtight container in a cool, dry place for a year or more. The longer they're kept, the drier they become, which increases their cooking time.

There is no need to presoak lentils. Before cooking, simply rinse them in cold water and drain well, pick out any debris or damaged lentils, and they are ready to cook. If they take forever to cook, the lentils have been stored too long and it's time to buy new ones!

Barley Risotto with Peas, Carrots, and Parsley

In this twist on risotto, pot barley (also called Scotch barley) replaces rice. Do not confuse it with the softer, faster-cooking pearl barley whose grain is more highly polished to remove the tough bran portion and the germ. Pot barley holds its shape better and will make a toothy rather than a mushy risotto. Spoon this dish alongside storebought rotisserie chicken or Sunday Dinner Rotisserie Chicken (page 33).

Prep time: 20 minutes • Cooking time: about 45 minutes • Makes: 4 servings

2 Tbsp (30 mL) olive oil

1 cup (250 mL) pot barley

1 small onion, finely diced

1 small carrot, finely diced

1 medium garlic clove, minced

2½ cups (625 mL) chicken stock (page 59)

1 cup (250 mL) water

½ tsp (2 mL) oregano

2 Tbsp (30 mL) chopped fresh parsley

⅓ cup (80 mL) freshly grated parmesan
   cheese

1 cup (250 mL) frozen or fresh peas

Salt and freshly ground black pepper
   to taste

1. Heat the olive oil in a pot over medium heat. Add the barley, onions, carrots, and garlic and cook, stirring, until the vegetables are softened, 4 to 5 minutes.

2. Add the stock, water, and oregano and bring to a slow, gently bubbling simmer. Adjust the heat as needed and cook until the barley is tender and all the liquid has been absorbed, about 30 minutes. (Add a little more stock or water if the liquid evaporates before the barley is cooked.)

3. Stir in the parsley, parmesan, peas, and salt and pepper and cook through for 2 minutes, until the peas are warm. Serve immediately.

Pecan and Cranberry Rice Pilaf

Pilafs first bubbled to life in the Near East, where they are typically made with rice or bulgur. To coat them so they separate easily once cooked, the grains are always cooked in butter or oil before any liquid and other ingredients are added. Serve this North American–style pilaf, which is dotted with pecans and cranberries, as a side dish with Sunday Dinner Rotisserie Chicken (page 33), Maple-Mustard Chicken with Coriander and Pepper (page 28), or storebought rotisserie chicken.

Prep time: 10 minutes • Cooking time: about 25 minutes • Makes: 6 to 8 servings

2 Tbsp (30 mL) olive oil

½ medium onion, finely diced

1 cup (250 mL) grated carrots

1 medium garlic clove, minced

2 tsp (10 mL) finely chopped ginger

2 cups (500 mL) long-grain white rice

½ cup (125 mL) pecan halves

½ cup (125 mL) dried cranberries

3¼ cups (810 mL) chicken stock (page 59)

½ tsp (2 mL) ground cumin

⅛ tsp (0.5 mL) cayenne pepper

Salt and freshly ground black pepper
   to taste

2 Tbsp (30 mL) chopped fresh parsley

1. Heat the olive oil in a pot over medium-high heat, then add the onions, carrots, garlic, and ginger and cook until softened, about 5 minutes.

2. Add the rice and cook, stirring, for 2 minutes. Add the pecans, cranberries, stock, cumin, cayenne, and salt and pepper and allow the mixture to come to a boil.

3. Cover the pot, reduce the heat to its lowest setting, and cook for 15 to 18 minutes, or until the rice is tender.

4. Fluff the rice with a fork, mix in the parsley, and serve.

Spanish-style Rice

This aromatic dish is similar to the Spanish-style rice served in many Mexican restaurants. Steaming the rice and infusing it with the flavors of onions, sweet and spicy peppers, spices, and a good-quality chicken stock results in a rice dish you'll want to keep digging your fork into. It is a good match for Traditional Barbecued Rotisserie Chicken (page 20) and would also taste nice with Jerk Chicken (page 25). Or serve it with Tex-Mex or Mexican-style dishes, such as No-fuss Rotisserie Chicken Enchiladas (page 105).

Prep time: 10 minutes • Cooking time: about 25 minutes • Makes: 4 servings

2 Tbsp (30 mL) olive oil

½ medium yellow or white onion, finely chopped

½ cup (125 mL) finely chopped green bell peppers

½ cup (125 mL) finely chopped red bell peppers

1 medium jalapeño pepper, seeds removed, finely chopped (optional)

1 garlic clove, finely chopped

1 cup (250 mL) long-grain white rice

1 tsp (5 mL) chili powder

1 tsp (5 mL) ground cumin

⅛ tsp (0.5 mL) cayenne pepper

1¾ cups (425 mL) chicken stock (page 59)

Salt and freshly ground black pepper to taste

2 green onions, thinly sliced

1. Heat the olive oil in a pot over medium heat, then add the onions, bell peppers, jalapeño, and garlic and cook for 4 minutes.

2. Stir in the rice, chili powder, cumin, and cayenne and cook, stirring, for 2 minutes more. Pour in the stock, season with salt and pepper, then increase the heat to medium-high and allow to come to a boil.

3. Cover the rice, reduce the heat to its lowest setting, and cook for 15 to 18 minutes, or until the rice is tender.

4. Fluff the rice with a fork, mix in the green onions, and serve.

Orzo with Asparagus and Almonds

Orzo is a small, rice-shaped pasta available at most supermarkets, and it makes a fine base for a side dish. You can make this side dish at any time of year, but I especially like to prepare it in the spring with freshly picked local asparagus. For added richness, pull 3½ oz (100 g) of soft goat cheese into small nuggets and stir into the warm orzo and asparagus mixture just before serving. Serve this dish with Sunday Dinner Rotisserie Chicken (page 33) or Spanish-style Chicken (page 23).

Prep time: 15 minutes • Cooking time: 8 to 9 minutes • Makes: 6 servings

1½ cups (375 mL) orzo

½ lb (250 g) asparagus, woody stems trimmed, spears thinly sliced on the bias

⅓ cup (80 mL) freshly grated parmesan cheese

3 Tbsp (45 mL) storebought or homemade pesto (page 169)

⅓ cup (80 mL) sliced almonds, lightly toasted (see Note)

Salt and freshly ground black pepper to taste

1. Bring a pot of lightly salted water to a boil over medium-high heat. Add the orzo and cook until just tender, 7 to 8 minutes. Add the asparagus and cook for 1 minute more.

2. Drain the orzo and asparagus well, reserving ¼ cup (60 mL) of the cooking liquid.

3. In a large serving bowl, combine the orzo and asparagus, reserved cooking liquid, parmesan, pesto, and almonds. Season with salt and pepper. Serve warm or at room temperature.

Note: To toast almonds, preheat the oven to 300°F (150°C). Arrange the nuts in a single layer in a small baking pan and bake for 10 to 15 minutes, or until lightly toasted.

HOW TO HANDLE AND PREPARE ASPARAGUS

Purchase asparagus with firm straight spears and tightly closed tips. They will taste best on the day you buy them, but they will keep refrigerated, sealed in a plastic bag, for up to 3 days. Wash the asparagus just before cooking. To prepare, hold the tip firmly in one hand and gently bend the spear until the lower, woody part snaps off at its natural breaking point. Discard the woody parts of the stem.

BREADS, BISCUITS, AND CRACKERS

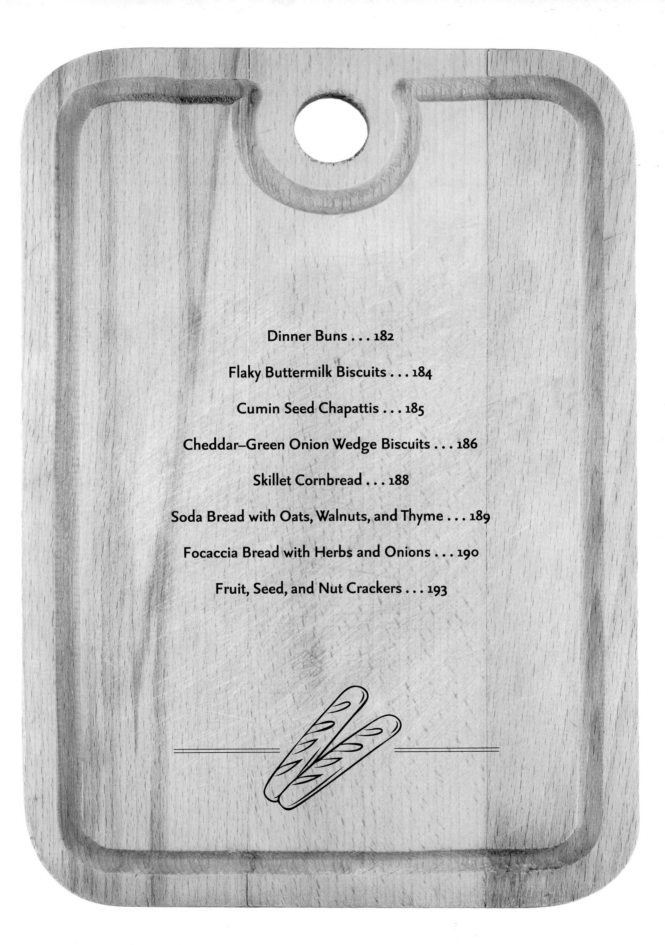

Dinner Buns

What could be more traditional than fresh-baked, soft dinner buns served alongside rotisserie chicken? White buns are usual, but for a whole-wheat version replace 1½ cups (375 mL) of the all-purpose flour with whole-wheat.

Prep time: 30 minutes, plus rising time • Cooking time: 18 minutes • Makes: 16 buns

1 cup (250 mL) lukewarm (not hot) water

2 tsp (10 mL) instant yeast

1 large egg

2 Tbsp (30 mL) granulated sugar

2 Tbsp (30 mL) vegetable oil + more for the bowl

2 ¾ to 3 cups (675 to 750 mL) all-purpose flour

1 tsp (5 mL) salt

1 large egg yolk, beaten

1. In a large bowl or in the bowl of a stand mixer fitted with a dough hook, combine the water, yeast, egg, sugar, and the 2 Tbsp (30 mL) of vegetable oil.

2. If using a stand mixer, add all of the flour and salt and mix on medium speed until you have a smooth, fairly soft dough that pulls away from the sides of the bowl. Mix and knead the dough for another 5 minutes.

3. If mixing the dough by hand, slowly add 2½ cups (625 mL) of the flour and the salt, working it into the yeast/water mixture with a spoon until the dough loosely clumps together. Lightly dust a clean work surface with the remaining flour. Gather the dough, scraping the sides of the bowl if necessary, and set it on the counter. Dab it lightly in the flour to coat it, then knead for 6 to 8 minutes, until a smooth, fairly soft dough is created.

4. Lightly grease a large, deep bowl with vegetable oil. Set the dough in the bowl, cover with plastic wrap, and allow to rise at room temperature until doubled in size, 75 minutes.

5. Line a baking sheet with parchment paper and lightly dust a clean work surface with flour.

6. Place the dough on the counter and cut it in half. Cut each half into 8 equal pieces. Using your hands, shape each piece into a round ball. Place the buns on the prepared baking sheet, about 2 inches (5 cm) apart. Cover with a tea towel and allow to rise for about 1 hour, until doubled in size. (It's okay if the buns touch after they rise.)

7. Set an oven rack in the middle of the oven, then preheat the oven to 375°F (190°C). Very lightly brush the top of each bun with beaten egg yolk. Bake for 18 minutes, until golden and cooked through. Serve hot, warm, or at room temperature.

Flaky Buttermilk Biscuits

These classic buttermilk biscuits are easy to make and puff up nicely. They pair well with Traditional Barbecued Rotisserie Chicken (page 20), Sunday Dinner Rotisserie Chicken (page 33), and Simple and Hearty Chicken Stew on Egg Noodles (page 116). You can also serve them with storebought rotisserie chicken. To make blue cheese biscuits, add 3½ oz (100 g) of fairly firm blue cheese, crumbled or pulled into small nuggets, to the dough when adding the buttermilk.

Prep time: 20 minutes • Cooking time: 12 to 14 minutes • Makes: 10 to 12 biscuits

2 cups (500 mL) all-purpose flour

2 tsp (10 mL) baking powder

½ tsp (2 mL) baking soda

½ tsp (2 mL) salt

¼ cup (60 mL) butter, cold, cut in small cubes

1 cup (250 mL) buttermilk

1 large egg, beaten

1. Set an oven rack in the middle of the oven, then preheat the oven to 425°F (220°C). Line a baking sheet with parchment paper.

2. Place the flour, baking powder, baking soda, and salt in a bowl and whisk to combine.

3. Using your fingers, two forks, or a pastry cutter, work the butter into the flour mixture until thoroughly distributed. Gently mix in the buttermilk until a loose dough forms.

4. Lightly dust a clean work surface and your hands with flour. Turn the dough onto the counter and shape it into a ball, then flatten it into a disk 1 inch (2.5 cm) thick. Use a 2½-inch (6.25 cm) biscuit cutter to cut the dough into rounds and place them on the prepared baking sheet. Gather up the scraps of dough, and press and cut them into biscuits as well.

5. Using a pastry brush, brush the top of each biscuit lightly with beaten egg. Bake for 12 to 14 minutes, or until puffed and golden. Serve warm!

Cumin Seed Chapattis

Chapattis are unleavened flatbreads eaten across India as an accompaniment to meals. Similar flatbreads are enjoyed in many parts of the world, including roti in the Caribbean and pita in the Middle East. These chapattis are flavored with nutty and peppery cumin seeds. Serve them with Tandoori Chicken (page 30), Jerk Chicken (page 25), or Chicken Tikka Masala (page 141).

Prep time: 40 minutes • Cooking time: about 10 minutes • Makes: 10 chapattis

1 cup (250 mL) all-purpose flour + more
    for dusting and shaping
1 cup (250 mL) whole-wheat flour
1 tsp (5 mL) cumin seeds
1 tsp (5 mL) salt
2 Tbsp (30 mL) vegetable oil + more for
    cooking
¾ cup (175 mL) + 2 Tbsp (30 mL) water

1. Combine the flours, cumin seeds, and salt in the bowl of a stand mixer fitted with a dough hook.

2. Pour in the vegetable oil and water and mix at medium speed until you have a soft, pliable dough. Knead the dough for 5 minutes. (Add a bit more water or all-purpose flour if the dough is a little too dry or too wet to knead.)

3. Lightly dust a clean work surface and your hands with flour. Using your hands, roll the dough into a log 10 inches (25 cm) long. Cut the dough, widthwise, into 10 equal pieces.

4. Shape each piece of dough into a small ball, and allow it to rest, uncovered, for 15 minutes. (This will allow the gluten in the dough to relax and make it easier to roll.)

5. Lightly dust your work surface and a rolling pin with flour. Roll each ball of dough into a very thin disk, about 6 inches (15 cm) across and ⅛ inch (3 mm) thick.

6. Heat a 10-inch (25 cm) cast-iron or other heat-proof skillet over medium-high heat. Add ½ tsp (2 mL) of vegetable oil and swirl to evenly coat the bottom of the pan. When the oil starts to smoke, place a chapatti in the pan and cook until blistered and colored with a few brown spots, about 30 seconds. Turn the chapatti over and cook for 20 to 30 seconds. Transfer to a plate.

7. Cook the remaining chapattis, adding ½ tsp (2 mL) of vegetable oil to the pan each time and allowing it to smoke before adding the dough.

8. Serve the chapattis warm or at room temperature.

Cheddar–Green Onion Wedge Biscuits

Moist and savory, these cheese and green onion biscuits are simply cut in wedges—no biscuit cutter is required. Create an easy, inviting lunch by serving these biscuits with one of the soup recipes in this book, such as Country-style Chicken and Cabbage Soup (page 61) or Chicken, Kale, and Bean Soup (page 69).

Prep time: 20 minutes • Cooking time: 20 minutes • Makes: 12 wedges

2 ½ cups (625 mL) all-purpose flour

1 Tbsp (15 mL) baking powder

½ tsp (2 mL) baking soda

1 tsp (5 mL) granulated sugar

½ tsp (2 mL) salt

¼ cup (60 mL) butter, cold, cut in small cubes

1 cup (250 mL) grated aged cheddar cheese

2 green onions, thinly sliced

1¼ cups (310 mL) buttermilk, mixed with 1 large beaten egg

1. Set an oven rack in the middle of the oven, then preheat the oven to 375°F (190°C). Line a baking sheet with parchment paper.

2. In a large bowl or in the bowl of a stand mixer fitted with a paddle attachment, combine the flour, baking powder, baking soda, sugar, and salt.

3. Using your fingers, two forks, a pastry cutter, or the mixer, work the butter into the flour mixture until thoroughly distributed. Stir in the cheese and green onions. Gently mix in the buttermilk/egg mixture until a loose, wet dough forms.

4. Lightly dust a clean work surface and your hands with flour. Turn the dough onto the counter and shape it into a ball, then flatten it into a disk 1½ inches (3.75 cm) thick. Lightly dust a knife with flour, then cut the dough in half, and then cut each half into 6 wedges.

5. Place the wedges on the prepared baking sheet, spacing them 3 inches (7.5 cm) apart. Bake for 20 minutes, until puffed and light golden. Serve warm.

ABOUT BAKING SODA AND BAKING POWDER

Baking soda and baking powder are used to leaven baked goods, such as biscuits and soda bread. Baking soda is pure sodium bicarbonate and needs an acid such as buttermilk to cause bubbles that allow baked goods to rise. Baking powder contains baking soda; a drying agent, which is usually cornstarch; and a built-in acid, such as cream of tartar.

Baking powder does not have the same leavening strength as baking soda because its active rising agent—the baking soda—is diluted with those other ingredients. That's why some recipes use a generous amount of baking powder or, in some cases, baking powder and baking soda to ensure they rise.

Skillet Cornbread

Make this cornbread when you want to channel the American South. Tangy buttermilk, mild green onions, and salty, spicy cheese provide flavor, and baking the cornbread in a skillet creates a pleasing crust on the top, sides, and bottom. Set wedges of cornbread alongside pieces of storebought rotisserie chicken. Or try it with Traditional Barbecued Rotisserie Chicken (page 20), Piri Piri Chicken (page 27), or Jerk Chicken (page 25).

Prep time: 15 minutes • Cooking time: 30 minutes • Makes: 8 to 10 wedges

1 cup (250 mL) cornmeal

1 cup (250 mL) all-purpose flour

¼ cup (60 mL) granulated sugar

1 Tbsp (15 mL) baking powder

¼ tsp (1 mL) salt

½ cup (125 mL) grated cheddar or jalapeño Monterey Jack cheese

2 green onions, thinly sliced

1¼ cups (310 mL) buttermilk

4 Tbsp (60 mL) vegetable oil, divided

1 large egg, beaten

1. Set an oven rack in the middle of the oven, then preheat the oven to 375°F (190°C).

2. Place the cornmeal, flour, sugar, baking powder, and salt in a medium bowl and whisk to combine. Stir in the cheese and green onions.

3. In a second bowl, combine the buttermilk, 3 Tbsp (45 mL) of the vegetable oil, and the egg. Add the wet ingredients to the dry and mix until just combined.

4. Pour the remaining vegetable oil into a 10-inch (25 cm) cast-iron or other ovenproof skillet and swirl to evenly coat the bottom of the pan. Set the pan over medium heat.

5. Spoon the batter into the skillet and spread it evenly. Transfer the skillet to the middle of the oven and bake for 30 minutes, or until the cornbread springs back when touched in the center.

6. Allow to cool on a baking rack for 10 minutes, then invert the cornbread onto a cutting board and unmold. Serve warm or at room temperature, cut in wedges.

Soda Bread with Oats, Walnuts, and Thyme

This hearty, no-yeast bread is leavened with baking soda (see page 186) and makes delicious chicken sandwiches. Slather the slices with mayonnaise, and top with lettuce, cold sliced rotisserie chicken, pickles, such as Fresh Zucchini Pickles (page 147), and anything else that appeals.

Prep time: 15 minutes • Cooking time: 30 to 35 minutes • Makes: 1 loaf

1¼ cups (310 mL) all-purpose flour

1 cup (250 mL) whole-wheat flour

½ cup (125 mL) large-flake rolled oats

1½ tsp (7 mL) baking soda

½ tsp (2 mL) salt

¼ cup (60 mL) butter, cold, cut in small cubes

1 cup (250 mL) grated aged cheddar cheese

1 tsp (5 mL) minced fresh thyme, or pinch of dried

½ cup (125 mL) chopped walnuts

1⅓ cups (330 mL) buttermilk

1. Set an oven rack in the middle of the oven, then preheat the oven to 425°F (220°C). Line a baking sheet with parchment paper.

2. Place the flours, oats, baking soda, and salt in a bowl and whisk well to combine.

3. Using your fingers, two forks, or a pastry cutter, work the butter into the flour mixture until thoroughly distributed. Mix in the cheese, thyme, and walnuts. Gently mix in the buttermilk until a loose dough forms.

4. Lightly dust a clean work surface and your hands with flour. Turn the dough onto the counter and shape it into a round, squat loaf about 6 inches (15 cm) wide.

5. Place the shaped dough on the prepared baking sheet. Using a knife lightly dusted with flour, cut a shallow X into the center of the loaf.

6. Bake the bread for 30 to 35 minutes, or until the loaf springs back when gently touched in the center. Allow to cool to room temperature on a baking rack, then serve.

Focaccia Bread with Herbs and Onions

Tasty homemade focaccia bread is easier to make than you might think. Make the simple dough, let it rise, shape into a thin loaf, and bake. Or make two loaves—this recipe doubles well. Serve it alongside a salad, such as Rotisserie Chicken on White Bean and Arugula Salad (page 81) or Tomato and Marinated Olive Salad with Chicken (page 84).

Prep time: 25 minutes, plus rising time • Cooking time: 25 to 27 minutes • Makes: 1 loaf (6 servings)

⅔ cup (160 mL) lukewarm (not hot) water

1 tsp (5 mL) instant dry yeast

½ tsp (2 mL) granulated sugar

1 tsp (5 mL) herbes de Provence (see Note)

1 Tbsp (15 mL) + 2 tsp (10 mL) olive oil + more for the bowl and the baking sheet

1½ cups (375 mL) all-purpose flour

1 medium onion, halved and thinly sliced

Coarse sea or kosher salt to taste

Note: Herbes de Provence is a blend of various herbs, such as thyme, rosemary, savory, and lavender, sold in bottles, tins, or bags in the spice aisle of many supermarkets and fine food stores. If you can't find herbes de Provence or if you prefer, try 1 or 2 tsp (5 to 10 mL) of a single herb, such as chopped fresh rosemary.

1. In a large bowl or in the bowl of a stand mixer fitted with a dough hook, combine the water, yeast, sugar, herbes de Provence, and the 1 Tbsp (15 mL) of olive oil.

2. If using a stand mixer, add all of the flour and mix on medium speed until the dough is smooth and pulls away from the sides of the bowl. Mix and knead the dough for another 5 minutes.

3. If mixing the dough by hand, slowly add 1¼ cups (310 mL) of the flour, working it into the yeast/water mixture with a spoon until the dough loosely clumps together. Lightly dust a clean work surface with the remaining flour. Gather the dough, scraping the sides of the bowl if necessary, and set it on the counter. Dab it lightly in the flour to coat it, then knead for 6 to 8 minutes, until the dough is smooth but still slightly sticky.

4. Lightly grease a large, deep bowl with olive oil. Place the kneaded dough in the bowl, cover with plastic wrap, and allow to rise at warm room temperature until doubled in size, about 60 minutes.

5. While the dough rises, heat the 2 tsp (10 mL) of olive oil in a skillet over medium heat. Add the onions and cook until softened, about 5 minutes. Remove from the heat and allow to cool.

6. Lightly oil a nonstick baking sheet and place the risen dough on it. Using your hands, gently press and stretch the dough into a thin oblong about 10 inches (25 cm) long and 9 inches (23 cm) wide. Spread the onions over the dough and sprinkle with salt. Allow the bread to rise for a further 30 minutes.

7. Set an oven rack in the middle of the oven, then preheat the oven to 425°F (220°C). Bake the bread for 20 to 22 minutes, or until puffed and golden. Allow to cool to room temperature on a baking rack, then slice and serve.

ABOUT FOCACCIA

Focaccia, pronounced fo-ka-cha, is an Italian flatbread that's incredibly versatile. Once you've made this version a few times, you may want try topping it in other ways. Below are two possibilities.

Tomato Olive Focaccia: Instead of sautéed onions, top the formed dough with 6 halved cherry tomatoes and 6 pitted and halved black or green olives. Drizzle with 2 tsp (10 mL) olive oil, then sprinkle with the salt called for in the recipe. Allow the bread to rise for another 30 minutes, then bake as described in step 7 of the method.

Slivered Garlic and Rosemary Focaccia: Prepare the dough, omitting the herbes de Provence. Instead of sautéed onions, top the formed dough with 3 thinly sliced cloves of garlic. Drizzle with 2 tsp (10 mL) olive oil and sprinkle with 2 tsp (10 mL) chopped fresh rosemary, then the salt called for in the recipe. Allow the bread to rise for another 30 minutes, then bake as described in step 7 of the method.

Fruit, Seed, and Nut Crackers

While bread of some sort is a more usual accompaniment for a chicken dish, these easy-to-make crackers make a nice change. Serve them with rotisserie chicken soups, such as Quinoa Soup with Chicken, Squash, and Pesto (page 72). Better yet, use them as a base for a snack or appetizer; for example, top them with a spoonful of chutney, a slice of brie cheese, and a few shreds of cooked rotisserie chicken meat. Start these crackers the day before you plan to serve them.

Prep time: 30 minutes, plus cooling and drying time • Cooking time: 70 to 75 minutes • Makes: 36 to 40 crackers

½ cup (125 mL) whole-wheat flour

½ cup (125 mL) all-purpose flour

2 Tbsp (30 mL) brown sugar

1 tsp (5 mL) baking powder

¼ tsp (1 mL) salt

¼ cup (60 mL) dried cranberries

¼ cup (60 mL) raisins

¼ cup (60 mL) currants

¼ cup (60 mL) slivered almonds

¼ cup (60 mL) unsalted shelled pumpkin seeds (see Note)

⅓ cup (80 mL) buttermilk

2 Tbsp (30 mL) honey

Note: Shelled pumpkin seeds are available at health food stores and in the bulk food department of many supermarkets.

1. Set an oven rack in the middle of the oven, then preheat the oven to 350°F (180°C). Spray an 8- × 4-inch (1.5 L) loaf pan with vegetable spray and line it with parchment paper.

2. Place the flours, brown sugar, baking powder, and salt in a medium bowl and whisk to combine. Stir in the cranberries, raisins, currants, almonds, and pumpkin seeds. Pour in the buttermilk and honey, and mix until just combined.

3. Spoon and pack the batter into the prepared loaf pan and bake for 35 minutes, or until the loaf springs back when touched in the very center.

4. Allow to cool for 10 minutes, then invert the loaf onto a cutting board and gently unmold. Remove the parchment paper, if still attached, and allow the loaf to rest on a baking rack, uncovered, for at least 4 hours or overnight. (This resting period will allow the loaf to dry a bit and make it easier to slice.)

5. Preheat the oven to 300°F (150°C). Line 2 large baking sheets with parchment paper.

6. Using a sharp serrated knife, slice the loaf, widthwise, as thinly as you can. Divide the slices among the baking sheets, arranging them in a single layer. Bake for 20 minutes, turn the crackers over, and bake for 15 to 20 minutes more, or until the crackers are crisp and golden. (Bake the crackers in batches, if necessary.)

7. Allow the crackers to cool to room temperature. Store them in an airtight container at room temperature for up to 2 weeks.

Index

Note: Page numbers in bold refer to photographs.